The Code

"THE CONSPIRACY TO CRIMINALIZE THE BLACK MALE"

An ancient Chinese warrior once said "If you know your enemy better than know yourself, you will never suffer defeat.

"This book honors those unarmed African American males who innocently lost their lives at the hands of law enforcement."

CS Inspires Inc.

Business Phone: 1-866-686-5836

CS Inspires Inc.
1837 Miramonte Way
Lawrenceville, Ga 30045

Website: www.thecodemyvirtualmentor.com Business Phone: 1-866-686-5836

ISBN-13: 978-1522864042
ISBN-10: 1522864040 -

DEDICATION

Dedicated To My Son
Cortlyn Jimmel Stafford

Son, all the conversations about manhood, character, and faith, were my attempt to warn and protect you from the looming challenges of growing up a black man in America. It is my prayer that I've lived a life worthy of honor and not demanded discipline, patience and perseverance of you that you never witnessed lived out when watching me. I wish you much success and a bright future limited only by your ability to dream, work smart and endure. I challenge you to unveil the KING in you and never fear the responsibilities associated with becoming the man God has created you to be.

ACKNOWLEDGMENTS

I thank God for introducing me to the love of my life. I am so fortunate to have you to love. You give me purpose. I love you for life, my wife, Patricia Stafford.

Cortlyn, all I have ever wanted was the very best for you. Keep pursuing your dream. I am so proud to be your dad.

I am eternally grateful for the sacrifices made by my late parents, Jimmie and Donnie Stafford. I strive every day to live a life that would honor and make you both proud.

Jeanette Gregory, my big sister, thanks for loving me for who I am. Your encouraging words mean the world to me.

To my cousin, the late James Williams, thank you for mentoring me through one of the most volatile periods of my life. You saw the best in me during the worst of times. I love and miss you Cuz!

Pastor John P. Kee, you will never know the influence you have had on my life!

CONTENTS

Preface

Outstanding leaders pass the torch with the fire blazing, Mediocre leaders pass a dimly lit torch. Poor leaders drop the torch making it difficult if not impossible to pick up again.

Reed Markham

PASSING THE BATON

The late Dr. Myles Munroe said, "An accurate measure of leadership is the ability to ensure that life's most valuable lessons are passed on to future generations before death." Shortly before his death, Dr. Munroe recalled dreaming he was at a funeral of a famous track and field star. He dreamt there was an easel next to a casket prominently displaying a portrait of this great man. Dr. Munroe recalled when it was his turn to pay respects to the fallen leader, he walked by and gazed into the casket and took note of the fact this commanding figure of success was lying there clutching a baton to his chest.

When he awoke, Dr. Monroe had an epiphany regarding the source of the greatest failure of current leaders. His assessment was that far too many leaders become so intoxicated with position, power and the privileges of the office, they fail to groom their successors. Similar to the track and field star lying in his casket gripping the baton, these leaders take the wisdom and knowledge acquired over a lifetime to their graves. Leaders with vision recognize by pouring themselves into tomorrow's leaders their legacy will shape destiny.

We have a crisis in black America. As a community, we are losing our young men in part due to the apathy of current leaders' willingness to mentor them. The consequence of our inaction is that the masses of black men are failing at the game of life. Black males rank among the most vilified, feared, maligned marginalized and misunderstood human beings on the face of the earth. The rich legacy of leadership attributed to our African lineage now stands in stark contrast to the plight of millions of young black males who have lost hope in tomorrow's possibilities. Far too many young black males have accepted they will not live to see their 21st birthdays. The cemeteries and prisons are full of black men with potential. The problem is potential without performance equals failure.

Black men are dying too soon, more likely to be unemployed, live in poverty and are disproportionately incarcerated in this nation's prison system. My clarion call to African American leaders is to unite around this noble cause. Our challenge is to equip a generation of black men to compete and succeed in a hostile environment for people of color we all know to be America.

I am reminded of a story a frog that was placed in a pot of warm water setting on an oven. Ladies and gentlemen, make no mistake; a pot of water on an oven is hostile environment for a frog. The frogs first impression was the environment appeared safe, warm and comfortable. What the frog didn't know was that the conditions had been designed by his arch enemy. The enemies' goal was to destroy the frog. The enemy understood the nature of the frog and hatched a diabolical plan to gradually turn up the heat two degrees every two minutes on the hour until the water came to a boil.

It would have been futile to drop the frog into a flaming hot pot of water because the frog would have recognized how hostile the environment was and leaped to safety. Inherent in the nature of the frog is the ability to normalize its body temperature to absorb gradual changes in the external temperature. By the time the pot came to a boil it was too late; it was too hot and the frog boiled to death.

Every day young black males find themselves adjusting to survive in a hostile social, political and economic environment here in America. America, from her inception was not designed as an environment conducive to promoting opportunities for people of color to flourish and succeed. Like the frog, our history in America has been filled with episodes when our oppressors have subtly turned the heat up on black folks with the goal of destroying the African American community. The destruction of the black male has been deemed central to dismantling the black family and ultimately marginalizing the achievements of citizens of color.

Traditionally black families were overwhelmingly composed of two parent households with both a mother and father present in the lives of their children. Family and communal values since our days in the villages of Africa have been the source of strength in our communities. Our oppressors hoped to dismantle the cohesiveness of our community replacing it with one that would breed distrust and infighting among our people. The strategy employed to achieve this goal has been to displace the influence of the black male within the African American community. The reputation and plight of the black male in America is not a coincidence; it's a conspiracy! Before the Founding Fathers of this nation's first thirteen colonies had formed a more perfect union, a diabolical plan had been contrived to disenfranchise the black male. The goal was to relegate black men to the lowest social, academic, political and economic rank among all of humanity.

Sadly shifting vales and dynamics within the black community have aided in fulfilling the plans of our oppressors. Today it's an openly accepted norm that black woman are playing the central role in leading most African American homes. Our oppressors enabled us to adopt family values they refuse to endorse themselves Today More than 74% of white and 80% of Asian families are headed by traditional two-parent households while within the African American community more than 77% of our families are headed by single black females. What has happen to traditional family values in the black community? More than 80% of black children are born to single mothers today. This cycle of dysfunction has bccn accepted by Generation X and the Millennials as *"The New Normal."* While I applaud the advancement and achievements of African American woman, our willingness to embrace and accept this unnatural and dysfunctional reprioritizing of the order and function of the black family has led to the demise of our community. We will deal with this subject in great detail in chapter four, "Dismantling The Black Man and in chapter six, Fatherless Communities."

Here are the facts; thousands of young African American males are growing up without the benefit of a positive male role model in their lives. While I commend black mothers for doing a heroic job at filling the void left by black men, she can never teach her sons the daily experiences of living as a black man in America. Thank God, the African American village has always stood in the gap and provided a network of uncles, cousin's coaches and segregates willing to extend a hand in raising our sons and daughters. The sacrifice of family and strangers was the key to my generation's survival! But there has been another shift in our communities that demands we alter our strategy in reaching a lost generation of young black men. We are more isolated in our homes than ever before. The villages influence has been marginalized as new generations are being defined as latch key kids who come home to empty homes and occupy their time playing PlayStation while bopping to the sounds of the latest Hip hop hits through their Beats headphones!

Generations of black males are silently suffering from the crippling effects of not having a father in their lives. Due to know fault of their own, these men are forced to struggle with the question of why their dads thought so little of them to leave them fatherless, unprotected and unloved. The absence of their fathers and the pain and sadness it has caused has taught them to bury such emotions; never allowing them to see the light of day. These men come off like Teflon Don on the surface but inside their hearts are hurting. The void for the affection and praise of their father eventually boils over into rage! Determined to blaze their own trail and make their own rules these young men often grow up hating their fathers and any male figure of authority that reminds them of their loss. He also has to live with the constant reminder that the one person he needed to teach him how to be a man denied him of this rite of passage.

During the late 1970s, game wardens in a South African game reserve decided to cull or thin out the elephant herds in one of their parks. The herd had grown too large and was disproportionately consuming and destroying the vegetation within the park. The wardens decided to act. Culling is a term used for euthanizing or killing targeted members of the herd. The practice is usually to kill off the giant male bulls!

After culling the herd, the wardens shipped two female adult elephants and 70 babies to a neighboring reserve. With no male bull elephants around, the young male caves unexpectedly split from the herd that was being led by the mother elephants. This was unusual because it occurred prior to their 5th year of birth. These young male elephants decided to split into their own little gang. It wasn't long before the wardens started to find members of the rhinos herd injured and dead. It appeared these attaches and murders were being conducted by this group of young male elephants. The wardens hadn't anticipated the highly complex norms that contribute in socializing elephants within the culture of the herd.

Within the normal maturation process the young male calves are weaned from their mothers around 15 years of age. The male calves then tend to travel more often with large male bull elephants. It is during this period they learn to model the behaviors of their male role models. The African bull elephant standing 10 feet tall an up to 7,000 pounds has the ability to control the aggressive male calves when they are in musth. Musth is period of sexual arousal marked by the demonstration of aggressive behavior by young male calves. The presence of the large bulls has been found to delay or reduce the time the young male calves are hormonally disposed to this highly aggressive nature. The wardens discovered the unpoliced young male calves in musth became violent and attacked and killed the rhinos. The young male calves lacked a male to control them while in musth and the outcome was tragic! I think you will agree the correlation between these orphaned male elephants and todays' fatherless generation of young African American males is undeniable. Young black men require order and structure and rules early in their lives in order to reign in their aggressive behavior. Young black males with no money in their pockets and too much time on their hands have a knack for finding trouble. These young men often join gangs or seek the admiration of the wrong crowd in quest of discovering where they belong.

The fact these young men have had to grow up on their own alters the way they see the world. Around ninth grade, the academic performances of black males tend to decline as they lose hope in tomorrow's possibilities. If you've ever had an opportunity to stare into the eyes of a 12-13-year-old black male from the hood you know what I mean. The icy glare in their eyes can be frightening. So much anger at such an early age! Around the same age momma begins to ratchet up her demands that he grows up and assume more responsibility. Her head knowledge compels her train him to be a man but in her heart, she feels sorry for him. She provides him a pass from the more rigorous duties out of pity and a desire to protect him from the impending harsh treatment he will incur when he becomes a man. Far too often mothers give in to the whimsical wishes of their sons, catering to every need, hoping he will grow up to become a better man and father than his dad was to him. Sadly, without structure and enforcement of rules these boys will mirror the bad behavior and choices of the fathers that abandoned them. The cycle continues!

It's a fact many of these young men have never witnessed a successful man model an honorable lifestyle before him. Can you imagine an actor being asked to recite a script they've never read? Most reasonable people would consider such a request absurd. Yet, we ask young black males to perform as mature men without training and mentoring every day. Without a mentor to model themselves after, African American males' failures become predictable events. Society then labels these immature young men failures. By this time these same young men begin to produce their own babies. The cycle then repeats itself!

Without a quality education and marketable skills, these young become trapped in the same seemingly endless cycle to become a respectable black man, unlike their fathers. Without good paying jobs, these young men like their fathers before them are unable to provide for themselves not to mention a family. Under pressure to live up to their responsibilities and be a so call man, frustrations drive these young men underground. Hustling introduces them to a subculture with an entirely different set of values and code of conduct. Underground these young men, with all their flaws find a place where they fit in and are accepted for who they are by the gang bangers, pimps, and fellow hustlers on the block. These young men then adopt the values of a subculture, where manhood is measured by how many babies they can produce not how many he can take care of and provide for. He is celebrated and accepted for playing the role of a breeding stud. Roaming from one woman to another having babies, he feels no obligation to nurture as his own.

I would argue these men would have grown up different if they were exposed to successful role models and a script to read before being thrust on the stage of life unprepared without, guidance, training, and practice. What if these men would have been provided an opportunity to role play before society expected them to perform as award-winning husbands, fathers, and men? When these young men make mistakes, the last thing they want to hear is condemnation without counseling, correction, and a cure! This book **"The Code" THE CONSPIRACY TO CRIMINALIZE BLACK MALES"** was created to aid African American males in navigating the social, political, and economic life skills required of them to thrive and succeed in American society. We cannot afford to lose one more African American male to the streets because of what he didn't know. In the words of Mya Angelo, "When you know better, you must do better. While the focus of this work highlights a uniquely black male experience; many of the principles are applicable to black youth in general. By no means should the focus on black males be interpreted as a disregard of the effects of not having a positive male role model in the lives of our daughters and the pain it contributes to their lives. This book does not diminish the physical and emotional wellbeing of our daughters but points to the urgency in confronting the challenges of young black males whose rage and blood are spilling over this nation's streets and prisons.

THE CODE GUIDE

- Every man needs a mentor in his life. Life is far too complicated to risk getting it right on your own. A mentor will share their life experiences and contacts to make your journey easier.

- Leaders pass on the knowledge acquired

- Young men need positive male role models to hold them accountable

- We become who and what we see in life

- If you are the smartest person in the group you hang out with; you need to find yourself another group

- You will become the average of the five closest friends in your life. Choose carefully.

- We as a community have an obligation to teach young males how to survive in this world

Chapter 1

Evil flourishes when good men do nothing.
Edmund Burke

THE NEW JIM CROW

Justice in America is not always fair! The Civil Rights Movement of the 1960's symbolized the struggle to correct the wrongs of this nation's past by renewing the promise of equality for all men, not just those of European decent. The mantra used in protest of the black man's second class citizenship during the days of Jim Cow was "I AM A MAN." Today in Ferguson, Baltimore, Chicago and cities across this nation, protesters have taken to the streets with their "HANDS UP" chanting "BLACK LIVES MATTER." This current voice of protest is to bring attention to what appears to be increasing disregard for black lives evident in the number of murders of unarmed African American males at the hands of law enforcement.

These crimes highlight the racially charged tensions black folks continue to be burdened with, more than 151 years after the abolishment of slavery in America. The criminalization of black men has become the modern day pursuit of right wing lobbyist and policy makers bent on reinstating free labor market systems practiced in America when slavery was the law of the land. The institutionalizing of slavery ranks among the greatest human rights atrocities known to man. Slavery also relegated blacks to the bottom of a permanent underclass **cast system.** The institutionalizing of slavery was inspired by greed for power, privilege, and profits! America's economic ideology has not changed. In 2016, there is a conspiracy to criminalize young African American males and exploit black labor through this nation's **Prison Industrial Complex**.

During slavery Southern plantation owners were able to leverage the benefits of a free labor market by exploiting Africans sweat equity to lower their cost and increase the profits they put in their pockets. Fast forward; the privatizing of American's prison system, the *New Jim Crow* of the 21st century, models slavery in that it profits from incarcerating an inmate population that is disproportionately black and male.

In 2016, privately operated prisons rank among this nation's most profitable blue chip companies, whose shares trade on the New York Stock Exchange, generating an estimated $70 billion dollars annually. Incarcerating African American males in American's prison has once again become a very profitable business model. America is the world's largest prison warden nation! While America accounts for only 5% of the world's population, we incarcerate more than 23% of the world's prisoners. African American males make up 41% of the 2.2 million, over 1 million black male inmates, in our federal and state prisons. How could this be considering the fact African American men only make up 6% of U.S. population? Blacks in total only account for 13% of the U.S. population. Leading legal scholars are unable to explain the extreme disparities in incarceration rates for blacks other than to acknowledge the obvious, American justice is not always just when it comes to people of color in this country.

While formal slavery ended on January 31, 1865, the systemic, institutionalized policies and practices required to maintain America's economic system by in large has remained intact. Chattel slavery, work contracts, convicts leasing, Black Codes Laws, Jim Crow and the current privatization of prisons all mirror each other in that under each of these institution's the exploitation of black labor is essential to the success of the economic business model. America expanded her global economic dominance by preying on African Americans, robbing them of the residuals due them for their investment in building what is the wealthiest nation in the world!

When I use the term America, I am not referring to all Caucasian citizens. I am talking about this country and our governments, social, political and economic policies and practices. Let's be completely honest America, white privilege does currently exist, and the color of one's skin still matters in this country. I also believe the recent heighten racial tensions point to the fact America has not adequately dealt with its racism problem. This country continues to administer segregated justice where the level of enforcement and the severity of penalties vary based on one's race!

This book was not designed to perpetuate the divisive name calling we have become all too accustomed. *The Code* was created to serve as a bridge to opening a productive dialogue regarding how we can tear down racial barriers that impede the progress of people of color. I also hope this book will serve as a roadmap, exposing areas of injustice in the American justice system in the hope that millions of young African American males will avoid becoming entangled in this counties *school to prison pipeline*.

THE CODE

THE CODE GUIDE:

- Slavery was born from greed for power, privilege, and profits!
- By establishing a free labor market, the Southern plantation owners could expand their operations by exploiting the African slaves
- Slavery started 160 years before the signing of the declaration of independence
- Several of the founding fathers of this nation owned slaves
- Slaves were bought and sold on the front lawn of the Whitehouse
- The institution of slavery has changed form but still exist in America
- The privatization of prisons is a blue chip investment business
- America warehouses more 2.2 million prisoners
- America accounts for more than 23% of the world's prison population
- More than 41% of America's prison population are African American males
- African American men make up only 6% of the society
- The criminalization of black men is big business just as slavery was for Southern plantation owners

Chapter 2

"Knowledge makes a man unfit to be a slave."

Frederick Douglass

MAKING OF A SLAVE

Approximately 286 years ago the first African slaves stepped foot on the shores of the Americas. These men and women were captured and sold like livestock into slavery to enrich Southern plantation owners. These plantation owners recognized the profit potential in exploiting free labor from the Africans to plant and harvest their crops. Unlike our European and Asian brothers and sisters, the *Statue of Liberty* did not welcome our African ancestors to her shores. The promises of freedom were replaced with chains of oppression and shackles of bondage. We were not extended the decency of being treated with the dignity due all human beings!

Unlike victims of the Jewish Holocaust, our African ancestors were not even afforded a true rendering of our history and suffering here in America. Prior to our arrival, more than 2 million slaves died or leaped to their deaths during the journey of the Middle Passage. During this six to eight week voyage across the Atlantic Ocean, men and women were chained to each other both wrist to wrist and ankle to ankle in the bottom of hot filthy ships. Those slaves who survived had to endure being chained to decaying corpses while sitting in feces the duration of the journey.

Upon the slaves arrival to America, Southern plantation owners and slave traders recognized that they had to defuse the rage and anger of the slaves or risk being overrun with uprisings. They recognized any form of organized protest would foil their plans to profit from institutionalizing slave labor. In order to stamp down the potential for large-scale slave revolts Southern plantation owners adopted a separate and distinct social code for managing and controlling its Negro population. The goal of this new social order was to break the spirt of the slave! This was accomplished by establishing a series of clearly defined rules designed to control and better predict the thinking and behavior of the slaves. These rules were enforced with swift and horrific retribution in order to strike fear in the hearts of the slaves. The African's first role in America was as indentured servants.

Indentured servitude was a form of debt bondage. Servants were almost always poor, but indentured servants were not always black. Their impoverished status was a part of what lured such individuals into this servant status. To keep the indentured servant in debt, the master increased the servant's financial dependence on him. The more credit extended to the servant, the more debt was accrued and the more time the servant would be required to work off their indebtedness. Over time, plantation owners determined there was too much risk in advancing the indentured servants credit as a business model. It lacked stability and often resulted in a plantation owner absorbing bad debit because a servant escaped and failed to work off the terms of their indebtedness.

I am of the opinion the status of the indentured servant was intended to be a transition point to adopting lifelong slavery. The indentured servant status was a way to socialize the first Africans who arrived in America and were sold the propaganda they would someday be free again as a result of working off their indebtedness. In the late 1640s, the colonist decided to terminate the indentured servant status. Moving forward Africans were considered slaves for life. Black folk would always be bound to slave masters not only by debt but through classifying Africans as property and not human beings.

The first 24 years of enslavement from 1616 to 1640 was no less than a test run for a more diabolical system that would consolidate government and economic policy. Wall Street, as we know it today, was built on the backs of slave labor. Billions of dollars were made, and America became the wealthiest country in the world! In less than a generation, slavery had been institutionalized and accepted as a normal part of American culture in the South. Of the more than 450,000 slaves imported from the African shores to America, 65% were males, 23% were women and 12% children. The population mix of the imported slaves was all strategic. The Plantation owners exploited men for their strength and their ability to work long hours in extreme heat in the fields. Women were assigned the dual roles of breeding with the African male slaves in order to expand the slave population as well as to contribute to production. Production for the women was typically as a field or house slaves. Most house slaves were female. Children would be trained to work the fields starting around 12-13 years of age. The ownership of large populations of slaves was considered a status symbol of wealth during this era.

Plantation owners determined that the slaves in their natural state (unbroken) were not fit for good economics. The Africans were accused of being lazy, unintelligent, and irreverent. Slaves were said to lack ambition and needed to be cultivated to extract maximum production from them. In the making of a slave, their culture, customs, and religions were stripped from them. The breaking process would consist of the following;

1. *The Socializing of The Slave To The American Culture*
2. *Destroying the Slaves Cultural Relevance*
3. *Controlling The Slave Through Religion*

The Socializing of The Slave To The American Culture:

Race would be a factor in who would inherit power, privilege and profits in this country. A **class system** was immediately formed that segregated people of color and of poor economic means from the social elite. The socialization of Africans into the American culture focused on differentiating the roles of those assigned to servitude and those occupying the privileged class. White's established themselves as superior to every other human in intellect, academics, economics, athletics, religion, war and sex. This required those in power, elitist, to revise history.

By eradicating the achievements of the subordinates, history would validate the insignificance of an entire culture of people, and support the myth white's had always been the superior race. It's important to note America was founded on the principles of elitism and white supremacy. The philosophy of **elitism** is an *attitude or behavior of a person or group who regard themselves as belonging to an elite group or class of people.* The Founding Fathers of this country were racial elitist. White supremacy became the dominant social, cultural norm. **White supremacy** *is a form of racism centered upon the belief, and promotion of the belief, that white people are superior in certain characteristics, traits, and attributes to people of other racial backgrounds and that therefore whites should politically, economically and socially rule non-whites.*

In order to sustain this new culture, Southern plantation owners determined it was of critical importance that they strike fear in the slaves in order to command their compliance. The inhuman brutality slaves were forced endure were barbaric in nature. Many of these practices were so vile I initially thought to omit including them in this work. Because our suffering is a part of our journey, I felt the truth must be exposed. I believe many of our unhealed and unresolved mental and emotional issues inherent within the African American community come from scars and trauma incurred during slavery.

We have hidden our scares ashamed to reveal our private pain. There comes a time when we must all face our giants in order to move past them. It's time we unearth some of the decaying bones of our past so we can properly dispose of some of the issues that continue to manifest themselves in our lives. Many of us suffer from low self-esteem because of our ties to ancestors' slave experience.

This hasn't always been the case; the Africans who were initially captured and enslaved were a proud people. The Africans were not accustomed to being abused and disrespected and, as a result, rebelled against the rule of their masters. Slaves would attempt to escape and destroy property among other tactics to show their displeasure with being enslaved. Whipping the slaves was a common practice. The master would tie them to a tree, expose their naked bodies and with force, tear into their flesh with a cowhide whip. These whippings were often administered in a central location where all the other slaves would be required to come out and witness this brutal punishment. A slave could be whipped for the slightest of supposed insubordinate behaviors. A man or woman could be beaten for not taking their hat off in the presence of a white person, which was thought to be a sign of disrespect.

One could also be beaten for looking a white person in the eyes or questioning their authority or God forbid, refusing one of their commands. A slave would be beaten or killed if they did as little as break a piece of farm equipment. Then there was a controlling mechanism called **"Buck-Busting**;" one of the most deviant, perverted, dehumanizing activities employed during slavery. Black males who were deemed defiant or strong-willed were tied to a tree and beat within an inch of their lives. When they were bloody and broken from the more than 30 or 40 lashes with the whip, the master would command other slaves or plantation overseers to bend the black male over a tree stump and pull down his pants, fully exposing his butt. The master was careful to assemble the slave's wife and children to watch. The offending slave's sons were placed front and center. The perverted master would then pull down his pants and openly commit sodomy on the slave for all to see. My blood boils just thinking about the physiological and emotional scaring imposed on those slaves who were victimized as well as those who were forced to watch.

I am enraged at the depths of inhumanity our ancestors had to endure for us to enjoy the freedoms we now too often take for granted. This act of performing anal sex on this slave not only destroyed him mentally and emotionally, but it also stripped him of his pride! Stripping the black male of his pride was the goal. To disgrace him and make a mockery of his powerless status was the aim of this brutal exhibition! This practice became so popular slave owners created **sex farms** where they could go and practice this perverted fetish whenever their flesh desired. Take note of how closely this practice resembles the practices of raping men in prison to gain control of new inmates?

Women were not exempt from the master's brutality. Because slaves were considered the property of the master, women did not own their bodies. It was a curse to be a beautiful black woman during slavery. It was common for white plantation owners to have sexual relationships with his female slaves. A female slave could be beaten or killed if she refused the masters advances. It was nothing for a white man to go to the slave quarters of a woman he desired and remove her forcedly from her husband's arms, to have his way with her. As for the children birthed out of these unions, they were sold off like any other slaves.

The slave mistress and their children were often treated poorly by the wives of the plantation owners who were angry about these openly sexual relationships. The wives often had the mistress whipped and their husband's slave children killed.

Destroying the Slaves Cultural Relevance

When the objective is to rule over people, there can be no credit or legacy of achievement attributed to them. That was the first in a series of steps undertaken by the colonists who took it upon themselves to rewrite history as it relates to the Africans. First, the African was stripped of his rich culture and legacy of achievement. Forget the fact that the oldest Homo sapiens were discovered in East Africa, the remains of an African man who lived approximately 200,000 years ago is widely recognized as the origins of man. Disregard the dark skin complexion, kinky hair and flared nostrils attributed to excavated Egyptians artifacts. It is undeniable there were once black Pharos who ruled Egypt; one of the greatest empires ever established. Why was so much invested in transforming Egypt, located in Africa, into a white metropolis?

Then there is the European image of Jesus the Christ. Its clear Jesus was of Jewish descent. Yet in the mid-19th century, as the slave population started to increase substantially in America, a modern white Jesus appears for the first time. Initially, he was depicted as a Jewish man with European features. Later, when the Ku Klux Klan wanted to indoctrinate the world around the superior race where blond haired-blue eyed people were to rule, Jesus's image was once again altered. Never mind the bible in the book of Revelations and how it describes Jesus's feet to look like burnished bronze and his hair like lamb's wool. Burnished bronze is a dark tan/brown color and lamb's wool; need I say more? Colonists chose to depict Africans as savages. The Africans names were changed to further confuse the slave and it was made illegal to speak their birth language! Eventually, the slaves developed a hybrid language with broken English becoming the core dialect used. The great enigma of the 21st century is that a fridge segment of the American population continues to deny the achievements of African Americans except those accomplished on the athletic fields and courts. In 2016, there is still this attempt to rewrite history.

President Obama inherited a country in political and economic free fall! Political partisanship had eroded before he took office but it was apparent shortly after he was sworn in as our 44th President the right wing political establishment was dead set on obstructing any progress he sought to advance for the good of the country. In spite of the opposition of his enemies, President Obama will be remembered as one of the greatest Presidents in the history of this country.

President Obama, as a two-term president, pushed through a national health care plan which has been a monumental first step in improving access to quality healthcare to poor and low- income people. President Obama also single handily saved the auto industry through his bold and unpopular decision to bailout General Motors and Chrysler. On the foreign policy front, it was President Obama who approved the Navy Seals strike that resulted in disposing of Osama Bin Laden who was directly responsible for the New York trade center attacks that resulted in the murders of more than 2,996 Americans. I'm sharing with you a brief biography of President Obama's achievements because the same political forces that chose to alter the Africans history in America appear bent on diminishing President Obama's legacy as one of the best if not the best President to have every held the office.

The tactic holds true, never to recognize the accomplishments of those you aim to control and to oppress.

Controlling The Slave Through Religion

I approach this discussion of religion in America reverently but with transparency and a desire to expose the truth. Within the context of socializing the enslaved Africans into American culture, religion became just another tool manipulated by plantation owners to control and predict the behavior of the slaves. The manipulation of religion by man is not a phenomenon. Since the birth of religion in the world, man has sought to inject himself into the role of the sacred. The God complex results in common men seeking to possess the wisdom, reverence, rule and authority fitting God alone! Wars have been fought, and millions of men have died in defense of individual religious expression. The African slaves were a deeply spiritual people. For thousands of years dating back to our native origins Africans practiced religion through ceremony, dance, rituals and customs. Our people have long practiced mystic beliefs in a higher power. Kemetic Orthodoxy, Voodoo and other primitive forms of sacred expression were the foundation of the African's core beliefs. Slave owners preyed on slaves by indoctrinating them with their own brand of religion, Christianity.

The plantation owner's motivation for socializing African slaves into Christianity was not completely benevolent. Compliance is required for any form of slavery to be sustained. Christianity was used to foster passivity and the compliance of the salves.

Slave owners and later Klan members clam to be divot Christians. Slave owners point to biblical scripture as the infallible word and will of God. Within their interpretation of the scriptures slavery was condoned in the bible. Slave owners taught sermons to the slaves that suggest they should submit to the will of God and accept their fate on earth. Slave owners claim to embody God's rule on earth. By positioning themselves as God's agent on earth the slaves were commanded to reverence and obey their masters as they would God!

Because the majority of slaves were illiterate, most lacked the ability to read and interpret the scriptures for themselves. Those who have read a *King James Version* of the Bible recognize the complexity of the text and the vast interpretive elements of the scriptures.

Their illiterate status rendered the slaves defenseless in engaging in discourse about the meaning and moral value of the principles they were taught. For many of the slaves, religion became an emotional expression based on the promise of freedom and a better life in the hereafter. The underlining message, obey your masters on earth and you will receive your reward in heaven. You may recall, teaching a slave to read or write was illegal. The master's words became God's voice in the ears of the slave.

The self-serving hypocrisy of slave owners becomes evident when you consider what they refuse to expose to their slaves. Politics and the right to vote and shape their own destiny was conveniently withheld from the slaves. Change demands revolution in the world of politics. The Founding Fathers of this nation knew this all too well, having to fight against the oppressive rule of Great Britain. By systematically eliminating blacks from organizing around the vote the slaves were rendered powerless to impact their destiny. This is a lesson to be learned from our past and a reminder of the importance of honoring those who sacrificed so much to secure us this right today.

It's a fact; religion has been used in the past and present to manipulate people. A part of our challenge as African Americans is to rise above the temptation to hate those who have purposely oppressed us. Hatred toward our enemies only consumes us in the process; denying ourselves of the right to hurt, heal and move on. Bitterness only keeps us trapped in the grasp of anger. We were debased in every manner possible as people but by the grace of God we survived. We survived not to take on the traits of our oppressors.

As black men we can no longer accept being studs, making babies we have no intent to father. Such behavior destroys the self-worth of the child and perpetuates dysfunction within the family unit. Our oppressors stripped us of our names to deny us our humanity, lineage, and respect. We cannot accept calling each other nigger and pretending the vile meaning of the words past never existed. That is the moral equivalent of disregarding the relevance and history behind the rebel flag. It's unacceptable to call our women, our queens, bitches, hoes, and tricks. Our job is to protect and uplift her not tear her down. If never before, now is the time for us to heal and move on!

THE CODE GUIDE

- The first African slaves were called indentured servants
- In 1640 African indentured servants become slaves
- These African's were proud men and woman who wanted to be free
- Slaves protested by trying to escape and through work slowdowns
- Plantation owners sought to control the slaves and reduce the odds of uprisings
- Owners used whipping and religion as instruments of control
- Buck Breaking was a vile practice that its effectiveness and popularity caused it to spread among the plantations
- Men and woman slaves were raped
- Religion was used to control
- Slaves were not allowed to learn to read and write
- Slaves were not allowed to vote

Chapter 3

"One of the great tragedies of life is that men seldom bridge the gulf between practice and profession, between doing and saying. A persistent schizophrenia leaves so many of us tragically divided against ourselves."

Dr. Martin Luther King, Jr.

DIVIDE AND CONQUER

When the Declaration of Independence was signed in 1776, the slaves were not included within their definition of humanity. The legislative bodies of the United States of America, while publicly proclaiming all men were created equal, in closed sessions, passed legislation stating the African slaves were to be valued as only three-fifths of a person.

What this amounted to was the newly formed government providing Southern plantation owners a tax incentive to increase their slave holdings and business enterprises. While it is understood the assigning of worth was more of a political move than an actual assignment of value, it was clear the first seeds had been planted to dehumanize the African slaves in America. The contradictions within the Founding Fathers words and their deeds were astonishing. One-third of the men who drafted the Declaration of Independence owned slaves. While promoting America as the home of the free, land of the brave, slave auction pins were actively selling human beings on White House grounds. Thomas Jefferson would eventually ascend to the highest seat in the land as President, and he owned more than 150 slaves.

By this time in our nation's history, the one thing that was clear was the vast potential for significant profits in the slave trade business and the colonists, and plantation owners would stop at nothing to extract their fair share and more. The one persistent challenge to their plan to institutionalizing a slave empire was the ongoing resistance campaigns by a segment of the slave population bent on escaping to freedom.

Black men were deemed the aggressors in this movement and were targeted as enemy number one by the plantation owners. The destruction of the African male's culture, confidence and character was intentional. The diabolical plans unearthed by these leaders and visionary minds were to dismantle the African man, his family and his traditions. The goal was to keep the black male in both physical and mental bondage, filled with rage, hate, and fear, for the rest of his life.

Slavery was created out of greed, not hate! Through a concept called cognitive dissidence, our oppressors were able to brainwash themselves in seeing the African as less than human and, therefore, relieve their conscious and justify treating the slaves inhumanly. **Cognitive dissidence** *occurs when a person holds two opposing values or thoughts in their mind and to ease the conscious they are forced to change their behavior or their attitudes.*

Example: A white father teaches his son to hate all black people. When his son comes of age he recognizes from his own experiences there are good black people. He is now conflicted over the two opposing values he holds in his mind. He must make a choice.

He can choose to ignore the false teachings of his father and befriend the blacks he has encountered or he can change his attitude and conform to the racist segregationist values of his father and maintain rank within his community. The slave traders and plantation owners were successful in designing and implementing a new social, cultural, political and economic model of governance. This new social political order fostered an economic ideology that would enrich the few while excluding the masses. Void of a true moral compass, they manipulated the human and cultural value systems, to exploit an entire race of people and distorted history and the Bible all with the aim of achieving a stable and profitable new world order.

The **Willie Lynch** letters provide a voice to this new world order. Willie Lynch was purported to be a plantation owner himself from the West Indies. Some question the authenticity of this character, but I will leave you to assess the significance and relevance of his writings. Mr. Lynch presents himself as a business owner, consultant, and trainer. His business was teaching other plantation owners how to manage their slaves efficiently.

Mr. Lynch was respected as an expert on this subject. The balance of this chapter is dedicated to reviewing the content and context of the Willie Lynch speech. We will be conducting an analysis of the implied and inferred meanings subscribed within his teachings. Please note Willie Lynch's complete unedited speech has been used and credited within my reference sources. The Willie Lynch speech will be transcribed in italicized bold text. Our analysis will be in the standard Times New Roman text.

As the story goes, a local group of Southern plantation owners and planters secured the services of Mr. Lynch. For a fee, he agreed to personally travel to the site and observe how they were conducting business. Like any good consultant, he agreed to review the current performance of his client's business operations and as a part of his compensation, train them on how to install his proven strategy for sustaining a rich and profitable slave trade in America.

Mr. Lynch's speech begins as follows;

Greetings,

Gentlemen, referring to the plantation owners and slave tradesmen assembled at this meeting, I greet you here on the banks of the James River in the year of our Lord one thousand seven hundred and twelve.

It is important to note, slavery had been taking place in other regions of Europe, and South America starting as early as the 1500s.
Mr. Lynch went on to say:

"I shall thank you, the gentlemen of the Colony of Virginia, for bringing me here. I am here to help you solve some of your problems with slaves."

During this period in America, the brutality toward slaves had reached epic proportions. Slave owners were fearful of revolt as the numbers of slaves continued to expand. There was unrest in neighboring towns and cities that compelled them to double down on their efforts to do whatever they could to maintain control, or they knew there would be a major uprising.

"Your invitation reached me on my modest plantation in the West Indies, where I have experimented with some of the newest, and still the oldest, methods for control of slaves. Ancient Rome would envy us if my program is implemented. As our boat sailed south on the James River, named for our illustrious King, whose version of the Bible we cherish, I saw enough to know that your problem is not unique."

Here we have a case of classic **cognitive dissidence**. Mr. Lynch refers to controlling slaves and their belief in the Bible all within the same sentence. Most would interpret the Bible as being a book that is supposed to challenge our moral and spiritual values. Mr. Lynch sees no contradiction in these clashing references and, in fact; many plantation owners used the Bible to justify their actions and attitudes.

"While Rome used cords of wood as crosses for standing human bodies along its highways in great numbers, you are here using the tree and the rope on occasions. I caught the whiff of a dead slave hanging from a tree, a couple miles back. You are not only losing valuable stock by hangings, you are having uprisings, slaves are running away, your crops are sometimes left in the fields too long for maximum profit, you suffer occasional fires, and your animals are being killed. Gentlemen, you know what your problems are; I do not need to elaborate."

Mr. Lynch establishes the basis for why the plantation owners should change their control methods. Up until this point, the hanging and beating of slaves were thought to be the most effective methods of controlling the slaves through fear. Lynching was carried out publicly so other slaves would be able to witness their fate for insubordinate behavior. Mr. Lynch was pointing out their tactics were not working. They were killing and crippling their property, the very source of their labor pool and as a result, losing money on the crops spoiling in the fields that were not being harvested. On top of all that, the slaves were still rising up, and burning and killing their animals, etc. The goal was to implement **psychological** war tactics to control the mind, emotions and behavior of the slaves.

"I am not here to enumerate y our problems; I am here to introduce you to a method of solving them. In my bag here, I have a full proof method for controlling your black slaves. I guarantee every one of you that, if installed correctly, it will control the slaves for at least 300 years. My method is simple. Any member of your family or your overseer can use it. I have outlined a number of differences among your slaves; and I take these differences and make them bigger. I USE FEAR, DISTRUST AND ENVY FOR CONTROL PURPOSES."

Playing the dozens or ranking is an art form and accepted pastime in urban communities and among professional comedians across the country. The very best comedians are skilled at drawing a contrast among people by blending truth and fiction all in jest. Within this lecture Mr. Lynch implies Southern slave-holders should employ the psychological practice of divide and conquer to create distrust among the slaves. This practice thrives by pointing out the differences in slaves as a means of aligning them on opposing sides. While I enjoy the cutting edge humor that's derived from this practice I understand the conflict and violence that can erupt when jokes are aimed at thin skinned individuals. To consider the origins of this practice may be rooted in the slave master's strategy to keep us at odds with each other is interesting to say the least.

On the surface comparing ourselves and joking at each other's expense seems innocent enough. What the slave master knew, by pointing out our differences and making them bigger than they were, it presented an access point to penetrating our personal feelings of self-worth and significance. Skin tone has long been an internal source of insecurity within the black community.

Slaves were taught the lighter the skin, the more attractive the person. Lighter skin slaves were given better assignments (housekeepers and servers) versus dark skin slaves, who traditionally worked the fields. The masters brainwashing strategy was to convince the fair skin slaves they were better than and more intelligent than the darker slaves. Many of us as black folks have bought into this madness hook line and sinker. We dare to look down own each other based on skin color. There was a time when I was young if a joke was made at my expense; I took it and kept it moving. If something hurtful was said you never wanted to let on it bothered you. Unfortunately, today a joke or the act of pointing out one's differences can result in a person being killed. Times have changed!

"These methods have worked on my modest plantation in the West Indies, and it will work throughout the South. Take this simple little list of differences and think about them. On top of my list is "AGE," but it's there only because it starts with an "a." The second is "COLOR" or shade. There is INTELLIGENCE, SIZE, SEX, SIZES OF PLANTATIONS, STATUS on plantations, ATTITUDE of owners, whether the slaves live in the valley, on a hill, East, West, North, South, have fine hair, course hair, or is tall or short."

To this day, many of the differences sighted in this section of Willie Lynch's speech have led to division and self-hate in the black community. With our history of slavery, African Americans are more insecure than most when it comes to our differences. Then there is the issue of the ranking of the plantations size and status versus another. Can you see the origins of gang turf wars? A ***turf war*** *is a colloquial term for "a bitter struggle for territory, power, control, or rights."* Today young black men whose only difference is a zip code and address are killing each other over turf wars, claiming colors and defending street corners they don't even own. Gang affiliation epitomizes a lifestyle rooted in q need to belong and self-hate! Did you know more than 93% of black males murdered in recent years were murdered by another black male? This has to stop!

"Now that you have a list of differences, I shall give you an outline of action, but before that, I shall assure you that distrust is stronger than trust and envy stronger than adulation, respect or admiration. The Black slaves after receiving this indoctrination shall carry on and will become <u>self-refueling and self-generating for HUNDREDS of years, maybe THOUSANDS."</u>

Distrust among the Brotherhood has been the source of great conflict in the African-American community. The African slaves were taught to trust, honor and respect their slave masters. A running joke was when the slave master was sick with a cold the slave would be heard saying "Sounds like we have a cold master." Slaves were allowed to fight among themselves but were met with swift retribution for harming a white man.

This distrust of each other has led to what many in our community refer to as the ***Crab in the Barrel Syndrome***. When harvesting crab, the crab as a group will pull down any crab that starts to climb out of the barrel in an attempt to be the first out of the barrel that holds them in, hence crabs-in-a-barrel. This practice is manifested when in poor and oppressed communities when one person tries to get ahead or get out of the barrel, jealousy, and self-hate within the culture results in the core group pulling that person down for fear they will achieve individual success and leave the masses behind. Such behavior thwarts the progress of our collective success. For example, other ethnic groups patronize their businesses and turn over a dollar five times before it leaves their communities.

Black folks spend almost 98% of our money outside our community and subconsciously feel validated as a result of being able to buy their brands and trademarked products somehow suggesting they are better than the goods and services sold by blacks.

I must confess to my error in judgment when it comes to this subject of distrusting and disrespecting a black owned business. Many years ago when my now wife and I were dating, I recall shopping for a dozen red roses for Valentine's Day. I went out of my way to patronize a black-owned florist in East Saint Louis. The fact of the matter, I lived closer to a major shopping district in a town called Fairview Heights. I was intent on shopping Black. When I picked up the roses, disappointment washed over me. The quality and attention to detail was lacking in the service and product provided. I walked out the door feeling cheated but instead of addressing my concerns with the owner, I vowed never to go back to this business again. Oh, yea, I also committed to myself I would tell everyone that would listen how bad the service had been at this establishment.

The first person I had an opportunity to unload on was my Alpha Phi Alpha fraternity brother Patrick Davis. He listened intently and let me get it all out of my system before he interjected. His first response came to me within a question. "Cornelius, have you ever received bad service at a majority owned store?" Of course, I said. "Have you ever returned to a majority business that previously provided poor service?" The answer was yes. He then went in for the kill. "Then why would you vow not to go back to the black-owned business when you didn't do as much as let the owner know you were not pleased with his work on that day. Why would a black-owned businessman not get a second chance? "My ignorance left me with no defensible argument. The truth of the matter is deep down in my subconscious mind; I expected the black-owned business would render me subpar service. In the same way, somehow I assumed the majority business owners would provide a superior product. This became a teachable moment for me. One I am ashamed to admit.

"Don't forget, you must pitch the OLD black male vs. the YOUNG black male, and the YOUNG black male against the OLD black male. You must use the DARK skin slaves vs. the LIGHT skin slaves, and the LIGHT skin slaves vs. the DARK skin slaves. You must use the FEMALE vs. the MALE, and the MALE vs. the FEMALE. You must also have white servants and overseers [who] distrust all Blacks. But it is NECESSARY THAT YOUR SLAVES TRUST AND DEPEND ON US. THEY MUST LOVE, RESPECT AND TRUST ONLY US. Gentlemen, these kits are your keys to control. Use them. Have your wives and children use them, never miss an opportunity. IF USED INTENSELY FOR ONE YEAR, THE SLAVES THEMSELVES WILL REMAIN PERPETUALLY DISTRUSTFUL.

Thank you gentlemen."

My personal experience is black men are far more violent towards other black males than we are with whites and other ethnicities. We buy into the economics of lack which teaches black men to compete against each other for a limited resource. I have personally witness black men and women take pride in being the only person of color in their company or department. The psychology of lack suggest to such a person only so many blacks will ever be allowed to penetrate the glass ceiling justifying feeling honored to have been deemed special in the eyes of their peers.

The slave conditioning within us demanded we love and trust our oppressors while suspecting the motives of our brothers. To harm a white person was an offense, punishable by death but black on black crime was seldom condemned and came with few if any consequences. I get so tired of trying to live down the reputation of being an angry black male. We have every right to be angry about the abuse we have had to endure here in America. The problem is we can't take 286 years of the master's abuse out on our brothers! No matter if the Willie Lynch letters are fact or fiction; there is much for the black community to learn from decoding the rhetoric of his speeches.

THE CODE GUIDE:

- Willie Lynch provided a strategy to perpetuate slavery
- The system was more efficient because the slaves were manipulated to become their own worst enemies
- By identifying our differences and assigning meaning and context to these condition masters were able to divide and conquer the slave families
- Joking about our differences can be hurtful, so it's important to know who you're playing with
- Slaves were taught lighter skin blacks were better
- Black are taught to operate from an economic ideology of lack which suggest there are limited resources and opportunities for success for people of color
- Black on black crime was allowed to flourish

Chapter 4

"There is nothing more dangerous, than an educated black man."
Anonymous

DISMANTLING THE BLACK MALE

On November 4, 2008, the former Illinois state senator Barack Hussein Obama became the 44th President of the United States of America, holding the seat of the most powerful man in the nation. A black man was voted into the most powerful and respected position in world government and politics! For many, this seemed to be the culmination of a dream that extended from slavery to the civil rights movement. Had America become a post-racial nation? Did color and ethnicity no longer matter? Had we suddenly arrived in a place and space where we were all truly free? Had a truce been declared against the conspiracy to criminalize black males?

Well, it didn't take long for this post-racial dream turned into a nightmare. There has ever been a time in this nation's history that the office of the U.S. President has been so disrespected. During President Obama's first term, Mitch McConnell, then head of the Senate Republicans said, "My number one priority is making sure President Obama is a one-term president." Republican Doug Lamborn (R-Colorado) said "Association with President Obama would be similar to touching a "tar baby." Worse yet, Congressman Joe Wilson (R-SC) during the President's State of The Union Address heckled him from the audience calling him a liar during a nationally televised speech!

The racist underbelly of America had once again exposed itself in a slightly different form with a slightly different message. Hate crimes have in fact increased Since President Obama took office. We are more racially polarized as a country than I can recall in my 52 years on this earth. The recent murder of nine members of Emanuel African Methodist Episcopal Church, in downtown Charleston South Carolina by 21-year-old Caucasian Dylan Storm Roof serves as a classic example of the expanding hate in this country.

Roof calmly killed nine African American church members gathered for Bible study. Mr. Roof sat in their midst more than an hour and was treated with nothing but kindness and latter admits while he second guessed it; he shot them in hopes of sparking a race war in America. Mr. Roof escaped from the scene and after being captured, the police in North Carolina stopped by Burger King to feed him before transporting him to the jail. Evil still exists in the world and incidents like the Charleston murders force us to ask the question, what is the price we must pay to rid the world of hate? Many have begun to wonder just how far we have come from slavery to the presidency of the United States of America. In the mean while it is important that we equip young African American males with the insights and strategies to better prepare him to defend himself and his family from harm.

The balance of this chapter is dedicated to revisiting another of Willie Lynch's more sinister speeches to plantation owners lecturing on his new and more effective technics for controlling the slaves. *The Dismantling of The Black Male* is the focus of this less popularized speech. All the more damning is his rhetoric which openly speaks of eliminating the significance of the African male within the hierarchy of the family structure within the African American community. Southern plantation owners recognized how brutal the institution of slavery was and feared retribution at the hands of the slaves for their unjust deeds would soon come. They would not give in without a fight and began to study alternate methods to break the mind and spirit of the Negro male slaves. They felt comfortable they could control the women and the children; it was the rebellious men that posed the greatest threat of revolting.

You will note the use of the original manuscript shown in italicized bold print. This script is a tool to compare and contrast the words and meanings associated with Mr. Lynches' claim of possessing a formula for changing the order of the black family by eliminating the significance of the black male. Willie Lynch systematically revealed the elements of his diabolical plan;

"We need a black nigger man, a pregnant nigger woman, and her baby nigger boy. Second, we will use the same basic principle that we use in breaking a horse, combined with some more sustaining factors. What we do with horses is that we break them from one form of life to another; that is, we reduce them from their natural state in nature. Whereas nature provides them with the natural capacity to take care of their offspring, we break that natural string of independence from them and thereby create a dependency status, so that we may be able to get from them useful production for our business and pleasure."

This reference to "**natural state**" speaks to a man's traditional leadership role and responsibility within the family. Men were created to provide and protect their families. Innate within every natural man is a desire to provide and protect his family and those he loves. Let's be clear about this, what he is proposing is to change the natural instinctive leader, provider and protective nature of black men to a more subordinate role within the family. Mr. Lynch speaks of reordering the purpose of the black male.

While the natural order of things would have been for men to be the leaders in their homes, such natural laws would be challenged under this new system designed to control African Americans. How so? The black male's character would be assassinated. Mr. Lynch's agenda couldn't be much clearer! The only questions that remained were what and how he would achieve this dastardly plan.

CARDINAL PRINCIPLES FOR MAKING A NEGRO

"For fear that our future generations may not understand the principles of breaking both of the beasts together, the nigger and the horse. We understand that short range planning economics results in periodic economic chaos; so that to avoid turmoil in the economy, it requires us to have breadth and depth in long range comprehensive planning, articulating both skill sharp perceptions. We lay down the following principles for long range comprehensive economic planning. Both horse and niggers [are] no good to the economy in the wild or natural state. Both must be BROKEN and TIED together for orderly production. For orderly future, special and particular attention must be paid to the FEMALE and the YOUNGEST offspring. Both must be CROSSBRED to produce a variety and division of labor.

The goal here is to break both the male and female so that in their new altered, unnatural state they will operate as a unit in perpetuating the will of the master. The will of the master was to use the male and female slaves to generate a profit and to be available for the master's pleasure. Here the plan is clearly revealed. The master's plan is to reverse the roles of the male and female in the African American community. The women would be elevated to the status of head of household.

The women would be responsible for providing and protecting the family. The black male's image would be tarnished by branding him as being emotionally unstable and fearful by nature and only good for producing babies as planation studs! Lynch warns this would require patience and a comprehensive installation plan to avoid extreme short term disruptions in their business model. The payoff would be a continuous regenerating system that would last for hundreds if not thousands of years once installed. Psychological and sociological gender role reversal assignment would be the specific tactics employed to control the slaves and destroy the black family structure.

"Both must be taught to respond to a peculiar new LANGUAGE. Psychological and physical instruction of CONTAINMENT must be created for both. We hold the six cardinal principles as truth to be self-evident, based upon following the discourse concerning the economics of breaking and tying the horse and the nigger together, all inclusive of the six principles laid down above. NOTE: Neither principle alone will suffice for good economics. All principles must be employed for orderly good of the nation.

The strategy must be implemented as instructed targeting all parties involved to include, the black male, female and youngest male son. The instructions were not to omit any of the principles presented to ensure a successful outcome.

"Accordingly, both a wild horse and a wild or nature nigger are dangerous even if captured, for they will have the tendency to seek their customary freedom and, in doing so, might kill you in your sleep. You cannot rest. They sleep while you are awake, and are awake while you are asleep. They are DANGEROUS near the family house, and it requires too much labor to watch them away from the house. Above all, you cannot get them to work in this natural state. Hence, both the horse and the nigger must be broken; that is breaking them from one form of mental life to another. KEEP THE BODY, TAKE THE MIND!

Here Willie Lynch exploits the fears of the plantation owners by suggesting the slaves were inherently dangerous and violent savages who at every chance given were plotting to murder their masters. The reference to breaking a horse is a subtle attempt to dehumanize the African slaves. The phrase "Keep the Body, Take the Mind" clearly communicates Lynch's theory that psychological warfare was far more superior to the physical beatings and whippings the Southern plantation owners believed would control the slaves. Not much has changed today!

"But, as we said before, there is an art in long range economic planning. YOU MUST KEEP YOUR EYE AND THOUGHTS ON THE FEMALE and the OFFSPRING of the horse and the nigger. A brief discourse in offspring development will shed light on the key to sound economic principles. Pay little attention to the generation of original breaking, but CONCENTRATE ON FUTURE GENERATION. Therefore, if you break the FEMALE mother, she will BREAK the offspring in its early years of development; and when the offspring is old enough to work, she will deliver it up to you, for her normal female protective tendencies will have been lost in the original breaking process."

Willie Lynch encouraged the plantation owners to focus their attention on the female and the future children. By focusing on the female and children, they would be effective in altering their natural state toward the black male. The plan administered correctly would ensure the female and children will alter the prevailing norms of all future generations. The natural position of the female and children will be transformed to unnatural, and the altered, abnormal state will become standard or natural. The only remaining requirement was to discredit the black male in the eyes of his female mate and children.

"For example, take the case of the wild stud horse, a female horse and an already infant horse and compare the breaking process with two captured nigger males in their natural state, a pregnant nigger woman with her infant offspring. Take the stud horse, break him for limited containment. Completely break the female horse until she becomes very gentle, whereas you or anybody can ride her in her comfort. Breed the mare and the stud until you have the desired offspring. Then, you can turn the stud to freedom until you need him again. Train the female horse whereby she will eat out of your hand, and she will, in turn, train the infant horse to eat out of your hand, also. When it comes to breaking the uncivilized nigger, use

the same process, but vary the degree and step up the pressure, so as to do a complete reversal of the mind."

The master's plan was to break the female and children's dependency on the black male as the provider, protector, visionary and instructor. In order to achieve this, access to resources for the black female and children must be associated with the benevolence of the master establishing a trusting relationship with the female slave. The master will focus on encouraging the female's independence from the black male and codependency on him. When the woman is fully codependent on the master and his system of control, the reordering of the natural order of the black family structure will begin to take shape.

"Take the meanest and most restless nigger, strip him of his clothes in front of the remaining male niggers, the female, and the nigger infant, tar and feather him, tie each leg to a different horse faced in opposite directions, set him afire and beat both horses to pull him apart in front of the remaining niggers. The next step is to take a bullwhip and beat the remaining nigger males to the point of death, in front of the female and the infant. Don't kill him, but PUT THE FEAR OF GOD IN HIM, for he can be useful for future breeding.

The brutality suggested by Lynch sounds unimaginable in the mind of a human person but in this case the motive was clear, to dismantle the African American male's character in the hearts and minds of the village where he was once respected and held in high regard. The tactics used in breaking his mind and body temporarily contributed to freezing him in a state of containment. Containment occurs when the trauma of the experience strikes such fear in the slave he abandons plans to rebel against the master. This provides the master a window of opportunity to further exploit the slave for the profits he is capable on generating.

By shifting the power and authority of the black family from the male to the female, the slave master was successful in altering the natural state of the roles and responsibilities' assigned to each of them by nature. (GOD) In so doing, the master became god like in predicting the destiny of the black family and the black male. While the black male was deemed suitable in the eyes of the master as a breeder to expand the slave population; his days in the role of leadership were numbered. Oppressors of our people have always been comfortable directing the activities of domesticated Negros willing to eat from their master's hands, and trust in his authority. But the socially, culturally educated black male, he must die!

The goal has always been to kill the spirit of the strong black man and replace it with a compliant Uncle Tom type, willing to tend to the masters fields for free.

THE BREAKING PROCESS OF THE AFRICAN WOMAN

Take the female and run a series of tests on her to see if she will submit to your desires willingly. Test her in every way, because she is the most important factor for good economics. If she shows any sign of resistance in submitting completely to your will, do not hesitate to use the bull whip on her to extract that last bit of bitch out of her."

The master plan has always been to displace the black male from his rightful place in his home and from his family. Once disposed of, those with evil intent were privy to direct access to the female. Testing her in every way implies assessing her strengths and weaknesses. The master must appease her so he can use her in their service. His goal is to get to know her and what her likes and dislikes are entering into a relationship with her and get her to trust them. When the plantation owners secured the confidence of the woman, they will have captured the affections of her mind, body and soul.

If she resists her master, he will be left with no choice but to bull whip her into submission.

"Take care not to kill her, for in doing so, you spoil good economics. When in complete submission, she will train her offspring in the early years to submit to labor when they become of age. Understanding is the best thing. Therefore, we shall go deeper into this area of the subject matter concerning what we have produced here in this breaking process of the female nigger. We have reversed the relationship; in her natural uncivilized state, she would have a strong dependency on the uncivilized nigger male, and she would have a limited protective tendency toward her independent male offspring and would raise male offspring to be dependent:

What the Willie Lynch letter is suggesting here is that the plantation owners must not become so frustrated and impatient that they resort to killing the female they have spent all, this time, cultivating as the new leader of the household. There will be great wealth laid up for the master when her children become of age to voluntarily spend their day in labor to help make the master richer.

He is warning that plantation owners should be careful to stay focused on the big picture. With the female as the new leader and head of household, the plan will have succeeded. Confirmation the plan has succeeded will be evident when the woman no longer looks to the black male for protection, but embraces her new role as "BOSS", capable of taking care of herself. In so doing, she will teach her daughters to be strong and independent so that they will be capable, like her, of taking care of themselves. The plight of her black male sons will differ from her daughters. Memories of the fate of her son's strong-willed father torment her. The memories of witnessing her once strong black man being beaten and torn apart suspends her in a state of perpetual fear for her son's life. She sees it as her duty to protect her son from impending danger.

She teaches her son to be dependent on her and he has become content resting in his mother's suckling on her breast as if he were an infant. Born out of her fear for her son's wellbeing and her desire to protect him she demands that he comply with the master's rules. She trains her son to be submissive so he will be perceived as less of a threat to their oppressors. He is taught to look away refusing to look master in the eye so as to never exert himself as an equal.

The warrior in him is feminized. Because he witnessed his father being sodomized, he's sexually confused. He lacks personal drive and has become dependent upon his mother for survival. Now both the male and female children have taken on unnatural gender assignments just the way the slave master wanted it to be. Now, this new species of strange black men and women are affirmed by society as being the new normal. Take note of this effective strategy for reducing the significance and respect of the black man in his home and community.

"Nature had provided for this type of balance. We reversed nature by burning and pulling a civilized nigger apart and bull whipping the other to the point of death, all in her presence. By her being left alone, unprotected, with the MALE IMAGE DESTROYED, the ordeal caused her to move from her psychologically dependent state to a frozen, independent state. In this frozen, psychological state of independence, she will raise her MALE and female offspring in reversed roles. For FEAR of the young male's life, she will psychologically train him to be MENTALLY WEAK and DEPENDENT, but PHYSICALLY STRONG. "

As discussed earlier, more than **77%** of black households are headed by single females. Generations of the young black males have never been exposed to the rich traditions of manhood. Somewhere along the way we have lost the intuitive sense to provide for and protect those we love. This altered state of mind plays right into the plans of those who would seek to destroy our sense of community.

I'm amazed to see the level of disconnect with so many men regarding the most basic values that we're ingrained in me as a young boy. It would appear many of our young brothers have abandoned the principle of true manhood taught when I was young. What happen to opening doors for significant other or mom? When did pulling out a chair for your girl become a sign that a man is week or henpecked. When walking down the street is it no longer common knowledge as a man you should make sure she walks on the inside furthest from the curb to ensure her safety. When did it become ok for the lady of the house to get out of bed to check for a noise or a potential intruder while the man lay in bed? Willie Lynch points to the fact the way to destroy the image of the black male in the eyes of the female was to destroy the perception of him as a provider and protector of the family. It's time to get back to the basics brothers!

While it's easy to point the finger at today's generation of young men, the real responsibility is ours to teach them. We cannot blame them for what we have not trained them!

"Because she has become psychologically independent, she will train her FEMALE offspring to be psychologically independent. What have you got? You've got the nigger WOMAN OUT FRONT AND THE nigger MAN BEHIND AND SCARED. This is a perfect situation of sound sleep and economics. Before the breaking process, we had to be alertly on guard at all times. Now, we can sleep soundly, for out of frozen fear his woman stands guard for us, he cannot get past her early slave molding process. He is a good tool, now ready to be tied to the horse at a tender age. By the time a nigger boy reaches the age of sixteen, he is soundly broken in and ready for a long life of sound and efficient work and the reproduction of a unit of good labor force."

The work is now complete! In this unnaturally frozen state, young black males will work for the scraps that fall from the masters table. The type of scrapes deserving of weak-minded high school dropouts who are willing to bend their backs and follow instructions to earn pennies when they have the potential to make millions of dollars.

"Continually through the breaking of uncivilized savage niggers, by throwing the nigger female savage into a frozen psychological state of independence, by killing the protective male image, and by creating a submissive, dependent mind of the nigger male slave, we have created an orbiting cycle that turns on its axis forever, unless a phenomenon occurs and re-shifts the position of the male and female slaves. We show what we mean by example. Take the case of the two economic slave units and examine them."

THE NEGRO MARRIAGE

We breed two nigger males with two nigger females. Then, we take the nigger male away from them and keep them moving and working. Say one nigger female bears a nigger female and the other bears a nigger male; both nigger females—being without influence of the nigger male image, frozen with an independent psychology—will raise their offspring into reverse positions. The one with the female offspring will teach her to be like herself, independent and negotiable (we negotiate with her, through her, by her, negotiates her at will). The one with the nigger male offspring, she being frozen subconscious in fear for his life, will raise him to be mentally dependent and weak, but physically strong; in other words, body over mind. Now, in a few years when these two offspring's become fertile for early reproduction, we will mate and breed them and continue the cycle. That is good, sound and long range comprehensive planning.

<u>WARNING: POSSIBLE INTERLOPING NEGATIVES</u>

Earlier, we talked about the non-economic good of the horse and the nigger in their wild or natural state; we talked out the principle of breaking and tying them together for orderly production. Furthermore, we talked about paying particular attention to the female savage and her offspring for orderly future planning, then, more recently we stated that, by reversing the positions of the male and female savages, we created an orbiting cycle that turns on its wn axis forever <u>unless a phenomenon occurred and reshifts positions of the male and female savages</u>.

An informed black male is the phenomenon racist Americans most fears. America has always sought to silence the voice of strong black men. Dr. King was once labeled by the FBI as being the most dangerous man in America for his stand against the Vietnam War. Muhammad Ali was stripped of his championship belt and band from professional boxing for refusing to comply with being drafted by the military to fight overseas for rights he couldn't enjoy here in the states because of his race. Malcom X was vilified by American media and labeled a racist.

Republicans declared President Obama to be the worse president in America's history in spite of all he achieved during his administration. This tactic fits the profile revealed in Willie Lynch's letter. Now is the time for real soldiers to stand and be counted if we are revers the trends that are destroying our communities.

"Our experts warned us about the possibility of this phenomenon occurring, for they say that the mind has a strong drive to correct and re-correct itself over a period of time if it can touch some substantial original historical base; and they advised us that the best way to deal with the phenomenon is to shave off the brute's mental history and create a multiplicity of phenomena of illusions, so that each illusion will twirl in its own orbit, something similar to floating balls in a vacuum."

The long-term strategy for plantation owners was keeping black folks confused and to cut us off from any knowledge of our culture and past and present achievements. Our strategy must be to ensure our children recognize the genius in blacks the like of:

- Dr. Martin Luther King Jr.
- Chief Judge Thurgood Marshall
- Lewis Howard Latimer created the light bulb filament
- Garrett Morgan – Created the stoplight
- Elijah McCoy – Built the first steam engine

Young people of color must know African American's have a rich history of achievement both on and off the courts, fields and stages of this country. We are more than athletes and entertainers and our history points this out.

"This creation of a multiplicity of phenomena of illusions entails the principle of crossbreeding the nigger and the horse as we stated above, the purpose of which is to create a diversified division of labor; thereby creating different levels of labor and different values of illusion at each connecting level of labor. The results of which is the severance of the points of original beginnings for each sphere illusion. Since we feel that the subject matter may get more complicated as we proceed in laying down our economic plan concerning the purpose, reason and effect of crossbreeding horses and niggers, we shall lay down the following definition terms for future generations. Orbiting cycle means a thing is turning in a given path. Axis means upon which or around which a body turns. Phenomenon means something beyond ordinary conception and inspires awe and wonder. Multiplicity means a great number. Crossbreeding a horse means taking a horse and breeding it with an ass and you get a dumb, backward, ass long-headed mule that is not reproductive nor productive by itself. Crossbreeding niggers mean taking so many drops of good white blood and putting them into as many nigger women as possible." The point here is to confuse the facts. Make it sound sophisticated so they won't ask questions. The real secret is to dilute the blood of the African with white blood, so the new Negro has little emotional tie to being black and readily conforms to the desires of the mainstream. "Varying the drops by

the various tone that you want, and then letting them breed with each other until another circle of color appears as you desire. What this means is this: Put the niggers and the horse in a breeding pot, mix some asses and some good white blood and what do you get? You got a multiplicity of colors of ass backward, unusual niggers, running, tied to backward ass long-headed mules, the one productive of itself, the other sterile. (The one constant, the other dying, we keep the nigger constant for we may replace the mules for another tool) both mule and nigger tied to
each other, neither knowing where the other came from and neither productive for itself nor without each other.

<u>CONTROLLED LANGUAGE</u>

"Crossbreeding completed, for further severance from their original beginning, WE MUST COMPLETELY ANNIHILATE THE MOTHER TONGUE of both the new nigger and the new mule, and institutes a new language that involves the new life's work of both."

By creating a crossbreed of African Americans, the slave master's plan was that our ties to African culture would become diluted over time, and our attachment to American culture, built on distrust, would feel normal to us. The Bible speaks of this type of phenomena in Revelation 3:15-16 NIV when it says "I know your deeds, that you are neither cold nor hot. I wish you were either one or the other! So, because you are lukewarm—neither hot nor cold—I am about to spit you out of my mouth." Passion is the key to success. Passion is hot! Lukewarm represents people who lack an emotional commitment to anything. They are more likely just to go with the flow. By diluting blacks with white blood, plantation owners planned to dilute the allegiance to African or black culture.

"You know language is a peculiar institution. It leads to the heart of a people. The more a foreigner knows about the language of another country the more he can move through all levels of that society. Therefore, if the foreigner is an enemy of the country, to the extent that he knows the body of the language, to that extent is the country vulnerable to attack or invasion of a foreign culture. For example, if you take a slave, if you teach him all about your language, he will know all your secrets, and he is then no more

slave, for you can't fool him any longer, and <u>BEING A FOOL IS ONE OF THE BASIC INGREDIENTS OF ANY INCIDENTS TO THE MAINTENANCE OF THE SLAVERY SYSTEM.</u>

Enslavement requires ignorance and compliance. The application of knowledge is power. The reason I am so concerned about the miseducation of black males is because it enslaves these men to the lowest economic class of citizens. When you're incapable of comprehending the language, customs, and culture of a society you increase your odds of being exploited.

"For example, if you told a slave that he must perform in getting out "our crops" and he knows the language well, he would know that "our crops" didn't mean "our crops" and the slavery system would break down, for he would relate on the basis of what "our crops" really meant. So you have to be careful in setting up the new language; for the slaves would soon be in your house, talking to you as "man to man" and that is death to our economic system. Also, the definitions of words or terms are only a minute part of the process. "

We can clearly see why there were laws prohibiting slaves from being taught to read and write. It made it easy for the master to lie to slaves without risk of rebuttal. Then there was the strategy of evoking such fear from the slave he or she would not dare question the master openly. The ability to understand the language and motives of others provide a clear message of intent. Oppressive people and environments thrive when ignorance flourishes.

"Values are created and transported by communication through the body of the language. An inclusive society has many interconnected value systems. All the values in the society have bridges of language to connect them for orderly working in the society. But for these language bridges, these many value systems would sharply clash and cause internal strife or civil war, the degree of the conflict being determined by the magnitude of the issues or relative opposing strength in whatever form. For example, if you put a slave in a hog pen and train him to live there and incorporate in him to value it as a way of life completely, the biggest problem you would have out of him is that he would worry you about provisions to keep the hog pen clean, or the same hog pen and make a slip and incorporate something in his language whereby he comes to value a house more than he does his hog pen, you got a problem. He will soon be in your house."

The goal of the enemy of black people has always been to eradicate the original values and cultural norms of our people. Dismantling the black male was required to gain access to the black family. With access to our families, the plantation owners of old and our current oppressors have the ability to influence the two most important institutions within black community: our village and our religion. With the disruption, our community lost sight of the values and beliefs that have girded us over a lifetime. In today's unnatural state, we are isolated from the village, and each of us has resorted to trying to survive on our own without the love and protection of the villagers.

Then there is our faith in a higher power. We have always been a very spiritual people. Our African ancestors practiced their faith daily. It was a part of who they were. Today, the Pew survey suggests fewer than 27% of the population attend church regularly. Young African Americans have fallen away from the church disheartened by the many wolves in sheep's clothing preying on the poor with profit, pride, and power as their major aims. God sees all and those who have defiled the faith and they will reap the seeds they have sown. As for the black man, the black female, and the black children, the Bible provides us a world of advice and encouragement.

Chronicles 7:14 NLT: “If my people who are called by my name will humble themselves and pray and seek my face and turn from their wicked ways, they will hear from heaven and I will forgive their sins and restore their land.

THE CODE GUIDE:

- President Obama's election as the 44th president renewed hope America had resolved its race problem
- Dismantling the black male has always been the goal of the institution of slavery
- All people and things have a natural order
- When the natural order of a God created being is altered it becomes unnatural
- Everything created has a purpose. When the purpose of a thing is unknown or abused, you will receive abnormal results
- The slave owner sought to reverse the roles assigned to black men and women
- Plantation owners planned that the unnatural role of future generations would be trained into the children through the women
- Girls would be taught and bred to be strong and independent
- Black boys would be bred to be physically strong and mentally and emotionally weak
- Ignorance would keep this system in place.

Chapter 5

"The Goal of The Oppressor Is To Control The Oppressed!"
Cornelius Stafford

BLACK CODE LAW IN AMERICA

Shortly after slavery was abolished in 1865, Southern plantation owners sought to reverse the effects of freeing the slaves. Their strategy was to enact laws and public policies that impeded the social, economic and political gains they feared would be made by blacks during this era. Local militias and police were the enforcing agents of BLACK CODE LAWS. Law Enforcement support of CODE LAW partly explains the ongoing distrust and hostility that exist toward police within urban communities today.

Most of these laws were far reaching, abusive and unjust, established for the sole purpose of controlling the progress of blacks during and after slavery was abolished. Examples of Black Code Laws are as follows:

1. Slaves were not allowed to learn to read or write
2. Slaves were not allowed to speak in their native language
3. Slaves were not allowed to marry in some states
4. Slaves were not allowed to possess a weapon
5. Slaves were not allowed to defend themselves against whites
6. Slaves could not seek a remedy in the courts against whites
7. Slaves were required to carry ownership papers on their person at all times when traveling off the plantation
8. Slaves could only work on plantations in certain jobs
9. Slaves were not allowed to own property or a business

Controlling the slave population was an obsession of Southern plantation owners who often feared the Africans would organize and overrun them. Over the years, many of the control mechanisms employed during slavery have evolved in far more subtle forms but are as effective in controlling the social, political and economic plight of people of color today!

Over the past 286 years, institutional racism has been promoted under the guise of any number of social and political movements: chattel slavery, the Black Code Laws, Jim Crow, the KKK or the mass incarceration legislation movement just to name a few. The means to the end of all these institutions has been to extract free or low-cost labor from a targeted underclass of individuals who lack the power or means to defend themselves. Even America's international trade policy, NAFTA was drafted with the goal of leveraging inexpensive foreign labor from Chinese sweatshops. The average labor cost for U.S. manufacturing is around $17 per hour. Chinese and Mexican workers, on the other hand, are willing to work for twenty-five cents per hour. Underlining greed has led to millions of American jobs lost to foreign manufacturing and a trade deficit that every U.S. President promises to balance before elected and somehow never ends up achieving when in office.

The mass incarceration of black men is not a new phenomenon. During the *First Reconstruction,* legislators enacted *vagrancy laws*. Vagrancy is defined as "The condition of an individual who is idle, has no visible means of support, and travels from place to place without working." When the 13th amendment abolished slavery in 1865, Southern plantation owners were forced to grapple with the lack of a workforce to plant and harvest their crops for free.

The enforcement of vagrancy laws resulted in the criminalizing of innocent black men, exploited for their ability to provide free labor through this nation's prison system. The 21st century equivalent of vagrancy laws would be sentencing homeless people to prison work camps for being homeless. The enforcement of the vagrancy law required once freed slaves to sign comprehensive labor contracts with those who once oppressed them during slavery. These contracts dictated where slaves could live when and where they could travel and the type jobs they could accept. These work contracts restricted and directed their ability to earn a living and threatened their freedom after the formal institution of slavery had been abolished. Those convicted of being in violation of the vagrancy codes were sentenced to harsh forced labor camps as punishment for this supposed crime.

The practice of convict leasing is another example of institutionalized slavery adopted by Southern plantation owners seeking to profit from cheap labor. State legislators contracted prison workers to provide labor to plantation owners and private corporations; in exchange, the plantation owners and companies were responsible for feeding, clothing, and housing the prisoners. Convict leasing was a lucrative business for the states. *In 1898, more than 73% of Alabama's entire annual state revenue came from convict leasing.*

Legislation and public policies of any type that support the unjust criminalization of black males represent modern day versions of BLACK CODE LAW. Within this literary work, I expose current laws and policies that reflect the spirit of Jim Crow of old based on the effects among African Americans. We will also share with black males, strategies on how to navigate the entrapments to the legal system that are destroying the black community.

During the Ronald Reagan's presidency years, the war on drugs and all of its associated laws, policies and rhetoric were in truth, nothing more than a modern-day version of the BLACK CODES. The war on drugs was a thinly veiled plot to incarcerate hundreds and thousands of black men by drumming up fear that drugs were America's most significant illness, requiring government intervention to eradicate crime by disproportionately imprisoning black men on drug law offences. The problem was more than 81% of the black men who were locked up were imprisoned for none violent offenses. Fewer than 1 in 4 men arrested were charged and convicted for trafficking drugs; most were charged with simple possession. These were not the drug kingpins shipping drugs into this country from Mexico or the far reaches of the world. In most instances these were street level users and hustlers who were in the drug game to put food on the table and shelter over their heads. Anyone who has ever lived in the hood recognizes the low-level trafficking of narcotics is a part of the underground economy of the community.

I'm not here to say this is right, but I am prepared to argue it's true. With unemployment rates double the national average in most urban neighborhoods, hustling is simply a way of life for many families who routinely struggle to make ends meet when there is more month than money. The real problem is the lack of jobs! Funny, no one wants to talk about the obvious problem. There is a direct correlation between poverty, crime rates and drug use in urban communities. While millions of dollars were being spent combating *The War on Drugs,* the real need was and remains today, programming and community recreational centers to occupy our youths time and employment opportunities that will teach our youth skills that will empower them to generate a lifetime living wage.

The war on drugs targeted local urban communities. Law enforcements focus on black communities; to the exclusion of majority white neighborhoods highlight one of the reasons for the disparity in America justice system. Study after study has proven blacks are no more likely to use drugs than whites. In spite of the facts, police have turned a blind eye to the drug abuses of whites, who represent the majority of American society. White privilege resulted in lighter sentencing and probation for the same or similar crimes where blacks were given stiffer and longer sentences.

The bottom line was, whites were abusing drugs at equal or higher rates with less consequence. During the peak of enforcement, federal and state agencies were incentivized based on the volume of arrest, not the quantity of the drugs seized.

The drug enforcement agent's assault on urban communities made for good TV with references to crack-heads and crack-babies addicted from the womb in black communities. The conspiracy to fight illegal drugs in the black community overshadowed the fact that behind the scenes, law enforcement leaders knew drug arrest were down almost 30%. The criminalization of millions of black males on drug charges resulted in them having their civil right stripped from them, eliminating their right to vote, secure quality high paying jobs and branding them as ex-con and felons for the rest of their lives. For those who understand how the system works, the label ex-con or felon can be the equivalent of a death sentence when it comes to a black man securing a good job! This was a devastating turn of events in the black community that led to thousands of fatherless homes in urban centers across this country.

The explosion in the number of black males incarcerated for drug crimes in many ways was reminiscent of the period in this nation's history when the original Africans were loaded on slave ships to be sold and exploited as free labor. For those of you who think the exploitation of slave labor is over, I beg to differ. Just as convict leasing stimulated state and local economies during reconstruction; outsourcing a workforce through today's prison system allows companies to profit from incarcerating American citizens. You just might be surprised to see the companies participating in this practice:

- Wal-Mart
- Nordstrom
- Eddie Bauer Harris
- Motorola
- Microsoft
- Victoria's Secret
- Compaq
- IBM
- Boeing
- AT&T
- Texas Instrument
- Revlon
- Macy's
- Target Stores
- Nortel
- Hewlett Packard
- Intel
- Honeywell

Now tell me again how BLACK CODE LAW and slavery is over!

BLACK CODE LAWS have now been replaced with CODE LANGUAGE! CODE LANGUAGE is as polarizing, but a more subtle form of racism. CODE language is laced with racial overtones without the emotional baggage of referencing race. CODE language sounds more clinical and less bigoted but serves the same purpose which is to demean and demoralize black folk.

Following are current forms of CODE language used every day. While race is not overtly referenced color and ethnicity are implied in the minds of the users:

- ✓ Welfare Queens
- ✓ Poverty
- ✓ Crime
- ✓ Food Stamp recipients
- ✓ Baby Mama
- ✓ Thug
- ✓ Ghetto
- ✓ Urban
- ✓ Drug Dealer

CODE language is also infused in legislative policy and socially acceptable phrases as well: Examples are:

- ✓ Driving while black
- ✓ Walking while black
- ✓ Stop and frisk laws
- ✓ Three strikes
- ✓ Profiling

These are just a few examples of how legislative policies have disproportionately criminalized black males by adopting language that frames most black men as suspects rather than law abiding citizens. We will revisit these legal policies, laws, and CODE language later when we discuss how to avoid becoming a victim of the criminal justice system. The miseducation of black youth is one of the greatest current civil rights travesties of our generation. How is it that the wealthiest nation on the face of the earth, capable of successfully sending a man to the moon and back; cannot address the current disparities that exist in America's education gap? We can no longer afford to turn our heads to this national crisis. America's academic institutions, once ranked among the best in the world, are now twenty seventh within the global community. America's permanent underclass is a byproduct of the inequities in educating black males. Nationally, 47% of African American males are graduating high school annually. When we focus on the performance of the largest urban schools in the country, the problem gets even worse. Examples; *Detroit, MI (23%) has the lowest Black male graduation rate in the country followed by Philadelphia, PA (26%), Clark County, NV (27%), Pinellas County, FL (28%), Cleveland, OH (28%), New York, NY (28%), Chatham County, GA (28%), Richmond County, GA (29%), Duvall County, FL (29%), and Norfolk, VA (31%).*

The relevance of this matter to the massive incarceration of black males is; African American men who fail to graduate high school are 70% more likely to serve time in state or federal prison. The school to prison pipeline is real ladies and gentlemen! The privatization of prisons is one of the most profitable enterprises in America. Private prison companies the likes of GEO and Corrections Corporation of America, have topped $70 billion in profits by offering federal and state officials a cheaper way of outsourcing the oversight of America's prison population. Why is the miseducation of and the eventual incarceration of young black males so important? Because current trends suggest failure to identify a solution will result in a lost generation of men who will adversely affect the socioeconomic standing of our country.

Today we live in a very image-conscious society.
In this post-civil rights era, one's worth is determined by measuring the accumulation of academic credentials, economic wealth and social status within the world community. The larger one's sphere of influence, the greater the power, privilege and profit potential accredited to the individual's status and rank. America has evolved into a modern day ***cast sys***tem segregating the haves from the have not's based on their personal resume and riches. Morales have taken a back seat to materialism. In this battle for supremacy, he who has the most stuff at the end wins! And then we as adults have the audacity to question why our children are so self-absorbed and feel entitled.
This elitist philosophy recognizes academic, economic and social status as the measure for determining individual success.

This definition of success has turned poor white people against African Americans and resulted in black folks fighting among ourselves. Why are we fighting? We are fighting for status and recognition by the elite of this nation. Everybody wants to be somebody. The Kardashians have built a financial empire by creating a lifestyle brand around fame and material success. Without a good reputation and high-level contacts, it's difficult for a black man to receive a break. Prison becomes the inevitable outcome for so many young black males who even with a good education and a good record struggle to get ahead in such an image-driven society.

This generation has made a mockery of the sacrifices of the Civil Rights Movement and legends the likes of Dr. Martin Luther King Jr., Former Ambassador Andrew Young, Congressman John Lewis, and C.T Vivian. Men who fought and some died for the equal rights of all people! Now, "Equality" which was the cornerstone of the movement, is being diminished in value. Legislators today argue *Affirmative Action Legislation*, designed to level the playing field for all mankind for past injustices is no longer relevant. This argument suggests we currently live in a post-racial society where race no longer divides us or even matters anymore when it comes to equal access to opportunities. This ideology also suggests there is no longer a need for set-asides to aid minorities in getting ahead.

We know this is not true. The demand for equal access has been misinterpreted as a plea for special privileges from a group of people societies successful citizens would suggest are hooked on handouts. If we are not careful the far right conservative wing of our government will overturn the gains made as a result of the 1964 Civil Rights and the 1965 Voting Rights Acts. *The Civil Right Act outlawed discrimination based on race, color, religion, sex, or national origin. It ended unequal application of voter registration requirements and racial segregation in schools, at the workplace and by facilities that served the general public. The Voting Rights Act of 1965 outlawed discriminatory voting practices.*

By neglecting to educate black boys, current trends suggest a steady stream of black males will help fund the billions of dollars generated through the Prison Industrial Complex. Some of the major contributing factors to these outcomes are as follows:

- ✓ Unfair senescing laws with longer and more severe penalties for minorities
- ✓ Systemic social, political and economic policies that favor preserving the current privileged elite
- ✓ Employment policies that discriminates against those with prior criminal records
- ✓ An unwillingness to invest in job training in urban communities

It's a fact; reviews completed concerning the sentencing process in America confirm blacks receive on average 20% longer sentences for similar crimes committed by whites. While there are sentencing guidelines, federal judges are provided the autonomy to deviate from the guide based on the preponderance of the facts as they see them. An example of the two faces of justice is revealed in sentencing laws on crack cocaine versus powder cocaine use. Until 2010 there was a significant difference in the penalties administered for crack cocaine possession versus powder cocaine possession.

Crack cocaine was the drug of choice for blacks and was more prevalently used in urban communities. Crack cocaine had far stiffer sentencing laws than powder cocaine, the drug of choice in rural and suburban communities.

Black males have been ranked the weakest link in a fragile chain of participants competing in today's global economy. I believe the new BLACK CODES are more sinister than ever. While we have made progress as a people, the masses of black folks and our communities continue to suffer from too little too late. While we celebrate the likes of Oprah Winfrey, Tyler Perry and a select few professional athletes and business leaders, the majority of black people, more than 286 years removed from slavery; rank among the lowest measures of economic success and the highest among most social ills.

Whites point to role models like Bill Gates and Warren Buffet as examples of how to acquire generational wealth, while far too many young black children continue to dream of becoming professional athletes and entertainers. As the former president of the DeKalb Chapter of the 100 Black Men of America, we sponsored an award-winning leadership academy. Our programs were geared toward providing young promising youth enrichment opportunities.

Our program was guided by a philosophy that by raising the level of expectation and exposing our youth to successful role models and mentors we could positively impact outcomes by transforming "C" students to "A" students.

During the screening interview process, potential students were asked what they wanted to be when they grew up. More than 60% of the incoming boys in the program expressed an interest in becoming rappers, NBA basketball or NFL football players. I get it! I was once there. Our youth aspire to become what they see. As long as mainstream urban media continues to glorify athletics over academics, we will continue to be faced with young black males who fail to grasp the social significance of acquiring a quality education. These young men will continue to be convinced they will defy the odds and be among the few to break the back of poverty through their participating in professional sports.

Parents, we are also to blame. Until we are willing to attend local PTA meetings and parent-teacher conferences, our children will disregard our insistence that they get good grades.

We can't continue to show up for Friday night football and basketball games and expect our children through mental telepathy to recognize which is most important. I am so proud of this book because of its focus on teaching black men specifically, and our youth in general how to thrive and succeed in a world that does not always embrace diversity. The goal is to empower minority youth with the wisdom that will prepare them to navigate through today's BLACK CODES! Education is the key!

THE CODE GUIDE:

- CODE LAWS OR BLACK CODES were created to impede the progress of black people
- CODE LAW provided plantation owners a means of controlling the activities and whereabouts of the once slaves
- The Founding Fathers never considered the plight of the slave when writing the Declaration of Independence
- The war on drugs under the Reagan administration was in truth a war on the black community. The incarceration rate increased 10-fold during the Reagan era
- In 2009 alone, 1.66 million Americans were arrested on drug charges,
- The graduation rates of black males from high school are a predictor of who will end up in prison.
- Black males who fail to graduate are 70% more likely to go to prison
- Those students reading at grade level by the third grade are four times more likely to graduate high school
- Convict leasing was a post-slavery movement to supply free labor to privately owned companies
-
- Privatization of prison is a $70 billion dollar business
- These private prisons contract with the government's federal and state agencies with occupancy rate clauses included in the contract which demands a specified number of citizens must be incarcerated to honor the contract.

The criminalization of the black male is the next phase of BLACK CODE LAW and policies adversely impacting black

Chapter 6

Parents can only give good advice, but the final forming of a person's character lies in their hands
Ann Frank

THE TALK

For centuries, black parents have felt compelled to set their children down and expose them to the realities of living black in America and around the world. The purpose of these conversations have historically been as is today, to protect and warn their children about the challenges they will face and the injustice they will likely encounter for no other reason than the color of their skin.

Today the practice of parents or guardians sharing the wisdom and insights of their past and the customs and culture of our people is more important than ever. The "TALK," as we will refer to it moving forward, in many ways symbolizes passing the baton. The intent of the "TALK" is not to perpetuate racial hate. The goal is to arm the next generation of youth with the life skills and cultural awareness to thrive and succeed.

Because of shifting family dynamics in the African American community, it is more important than ever for young African American males to be exposed to positive black male role models to speak into their lives. Three years ago I became aware of this demand when as President of the 100 Black Men of DeKalb County, GA; on a daily basis I would receive emails and phone calls from parents and guardians requesting a mentor for their young sons. While our Leadership Academy served both males and females I seldom recall receiving inquiries seeking assistance for their daughters; it was their sons that were at risk. The average age of the child in need of support was between 13-15 years old.

Unfortunately, even at this early age, most of these young men had already been faced with disciplinary and academic challenges in school. While we would have loved to serve every child, the lack of adequate resources and manpower would not allow. Thus, the "Virtual Mentor" was birthed! (www.thecodemyvirtualmentor.com)

Mentor, a national organization, committed to connecting youth and caring adults conducted a recent survey, where more than 17.6 million American youth said they would like to have a mentor. Of the more than four thousand organizations that service this need, only 4 million young people are being exposed to formally structured programming. That leaves more than 14.6 million youth without the benefits of a mentor in their lives. The "Virtual Mentoring's" primary focus is to provide a source of youth engagement and dialogue by leveraging technology in a virtual world. Most activities are accessible online, but live events are also a part of the programming. This book, workbook and audio program are a part of the curriculum of the "Virtual Mentoring Program." The programming design and services offered allow the mentees to maintain an ongoing connection with mentors who expose them to elements of their history, culture, critical life skills and etiquette training that will prepare them for success.

The "Virtual Mentor" was created as a result of the influence of my mother, the late Donnie V. Stafford, who I witnessed mentor friends and members of our family on a weekly basis. I can remember her brother, my uncle Willie Martin and her nephew, my cousin James Williams sitting around talking for hours at a time about life's issues. These were never heated debates, always calm and respectful conversations filled with vibrant and varied life experiences. They trusted each other and were able to be transparent with each other. We all would be only so lucky to have someone we could pour out our souls to and know our words and our sorted past would not be held against us later. Today we have lost touch with who our neighbors and network are. We have become isolated from each other. The "Virtual Mentor" restores the concept "It takes a village to raise our children." The "Virtual Mentor represents our ongoing effort beyond reading this book to engage our youth. I encourage you to take the time to log into the Virtual Mentor website and join the movement to save our black males.

THE CODE

I remember when I was around ten years of age living in the Roosevelt Homes, a housing project in East Saint Louis. I didn't know it then; but in terms of time spent with good friends and family, those were among the best times of my life. While we were considered poor, we were abundantly rich in the friendships and relationships that formed our immediate and extended family. Unlike today, then we knew our neighbors. If I got out of line, Mrs. Jones, my friend Kerry's mother or Mrs. Ethel my friend Darryl's grandmother could call me on it, and neither of them had a problem going to my mom and dad to ensure the message got home. The village helped raise me! We did not have much in the way of material wealth individually but collectively; we always had enough. If we needed sugar and Mrs. Ethel needed flour, we shared with each other, and everyone ate cake that evening. Everyone in the neighborhood committed themselves to doing their part to make sure the kids in the community stayed grounded and were aware of the challenges and the obstacles looming just beyond the poorly lite street corners of 42nd and Caseyville Ave where we lived.

At a point in our cultural history, black folks experienced a breakdown in our sense of community. We abandoned many of the tried and true principles that transformed our neighborhoods into a village of concerned citizens who all shared in raising our children. This breakdown has led to the demise of the sense of community that once helped facilitate the conversations that created the bonds that forged our collective commitments to be "Our Brothers Keepers," on a daily basis. The big losers have been our youth!

Today's media exposes our youth to more negative messages by the age of eight than my generations were exposed to by eighteen. Many of these negative messages are leading our young people to their destruction. Our young people in general and our males specifically need a survival guide or a blueprint to increase the odds they will make it home safe at night. The black community lost the moral compass that had guided us through the most tumultuous periods of our history. This literary work is my attempt to restore the voice of the village. The wisdom of the elders was and remains the most valuable asset of the community.

As we move forward, I will share some of the most important cultural, moral, social values that have guided the back community and been a part of the rich legacy passed down through the ages by the elders to keep our children safe and to prepare them for success.

The Stresses of Living Black:

America has criminalized the image of black males. Most black men will tell you even if you are a brother trying to do the right thing; much of white society will still brand you as a thug! The label thus places an unfair obligation on black men to always prove our innocence. This demand that black men always prove their innocence is a source of silent stress. This one fact alone creates a constant stress point that black men have to be taught to deal with throughout their lives. The feeling of always being scrutinized or marginalized can be a weighty burden to bear. If not prepared, society's response based on fears and stereotypes come off insensitive and insulting. The simple task of catching a taxi cab can be a humiliating daily routine for a black man. Taxi drivers have been known to pass on servicing black males for any number of stereotypical reasons that enable them to justify such crude and despicable behavior.

This suffocating existence leaves little room for exuberant self-expression or justifiable anger without suffering the consequence of being labeled arrogant or worse yet an angry black man! The hypocrisy and indifference of America toward young black men has never been more evident than in the ridicule hurled at Carolina Panthers star quarterback Cameron Newton and Seattle Seahawks All-Pro cornerback Richard Sherman. Cam Newton, coming off a 2016 NFL MVP performance season when asked why he is viewed as such a polarizing figure among fans and players for his elaborate touchdown celebrations and confident disposition responded, "Because I am an African American male, and they don't understand me and my culture." Cam's words could never be truer. Green Bay Packers quarterback Aron Rodgers has made his "Double Check" hip thrusting dance after scoring touchdowns a marketing phenomenon.

Aron Rodgers was awarded a multi-million dollar endorsement deal by State Farm Insurance, which airs a series of "Double Check" commercials daily around the world. Why is it, Mr. Rodgers is not is considered a polarizing figure?

Richard Sherman, a Stanford University graduate who also happens to be recognized as one of the best cornerbacks ever to play in the NFL also has a reputation for being polarizing. Why? Richard is known around the league for his trash talking antics on and off the field. I can only express how disappointing it was to hear the supposedly seasoned professional play by play commentators and reports refer to Mr. Sherman as a thug! I've never heard the legendary former Chicago Bears football coach Mike Ditka or Rex Ryan, coach of the Buffalo Bills, both major trash talkers in their own right, referred to as thugs!

Then there is the other end of the emotional scale when assessing the Republican Blue Collar wings disdain for President Obama. President Obama never seems rattled and often very measured and stoic in his outward persona. President Obama political nickname is "*no drama Obama*," suggestive of his pragmatic emotionless demeanor. I must admit; this personality has been the source of great pride and frustration for outspoken individuals like me. There have been times when his composure under fire appeared unnatural. On more than one occasion I found myself screaming into the television, "Defend Yourself." What I came to understand was as this nation's first black President, Obama has had to avoid the possibility of being labeled an angry or emotional black man. However unnatural it appeared, I privately understood the social conditions that confined the range of normal human emotions allowed to be expressed by a black man in America. President Obama has had to play by a different set of rules. The source of frustration and stress is watching current Republican presidential candidate Donald Trump breaks every politically correct rule in the book but remain the front runner and likely Republican candidate in his bid for the White House. Unfortunately this points to another area where there is a double standard for whites.

I remember being told over and over as a young black man, you must work twice as hard to receive fair consideration and an opportunity to be successful when competing against your white peers. It's a sad reality; to successfully integrate into society, African American males must prove they are not angry or violent to be trusted. If not taught to balance these dynamics within his daily reality by a Mentor, one runs the risk of becoming a "Domesticated Negro," who incessantly smiles when nothing is funny and scratch where he does not itch, all with the intent of getting along. In the end, far too many black males conclude the tradeoff is to be liked over being respected a distinction that compromises his dignity and his ability to compete and win when paired with his white peers!

There is nothing worse than a passive feminized male who lacks a voice and integrity within his peer group.

THE DOUBLE STANDARDS OF LIVING BLACK:

There is always a desire to protect the innocence of our children. Sharing the vile realities of a racially polarized, sometimes unjust society is not something African Americans want to expose to their young sons and daughters. Between 12 and 15 years of age, most parents of black adolescent boys recognize the need to have those first conversations about social etiquette and the image and challenges unique to black males. Like clockwork, around this age young African American males transform from smiley-faced fun-loving young men to hardened, angry, disenfranchised misunderstood, terminal minded victims of society. What most don't understand is the fact these young men are reacting to their environment and the conditions that affect their small world.

This period defines the time when young black males become socially aware that they are different. This is when black males become aware they are not accepted by society and that apparent double standards exist in how he will be treated on a daily basis.

Most males are territorial. Male Lyons for example, the kings of the jungle, mark their territory by urinating along the boundaries of what he claims to be his turf. Young black men learn the consequences of being labeled a predator or prey. While the goal is to avoid a fight, when required to defend one's self the goal must be to win. Young black men use nonverbal communication or what we call mean mugging as his way of conveying the message don't invade my space! His outward physical posture intentionally infers don't mess with me! His aggressive response is derived from a protective impulse to survive and to conceal his human frailties. This is where the value of a good mentor who can have the "TALK" with this young man comes to play. To tell this young man to put a smile on his face and be happy defies his nature. He is a warrior at heart. When he feels under attack, he is wired to fight and if necessary to die protecting his turf!

What this young man must be taught is how to balance his passion with his compassion for the dignity of all human life. Black males must be taught how to build relationships that enable him to lower their external threat alarm to a level that will enable them to build lasting and trusting relationships with people who may not look like him or share their same values or experiences. A mature black male realizes the goal of social interaction is not to conform into someone they're not but to minimize the threats associated with who they are.

The real problem is while the young African American male is marking his territory; society has already profiled him as a thug, a menace to society, seeking revenge on all white people. This is simply not true. His physical size makes him intimidating as he matures. Evidence of this, he starts to notice white women walking to the other side of the street when he nears them. The Asian lady on the elevator clutches her purse when he enters. When he walks past a car waiting at the traffic light, the passengers lock their doors. Over time, this type of response to his presence hardens the young man's perception of the world around him and adversely impacts his self-perception and ultimately his self-worth.

LIVING TO FIGHT ANOTHER DAY:

My wife and I recently celebrated the 21st birthday of our one and only son. Like most parents, we love our son and pray that he will grow up to be a responsible and successful member of society. While we are proud of the young man he has become, like millions of African American parents, we sometimes worry that he could become mixed up in some random incident and lose his life for any number of pointless reasons. Every time our son leaves the house, my wife and I subconsciously whisper a brief prayer over him asking God to cover, protect and bring him back to us safe.

Releasing our children to the world can be a traumatic experience. We hope as parents and mentors we have prepared them to stand on their own two feet, yet, there is always that glimmer of doubt that causes us to second guess if they can navigate life's heartaches, disappointments, and setbacks without us. In the end, we are forced to rely on what we have taught them to carry them through the highs and lows of their lives.

RULES OF SOCIAL ENGAGEMENT:

Selecting ones network of friends is a crucial factor in predicting our future success. If I heard it once I've heard it a thousand times," watch the company you keep." Parents typically have an acute sixth sense in sifting out those friends who are good or bad for us. Also, because they know us so well, our parents recognize when we are acting out of character and under the influence of someone else's agenda. Unfortunately, all it takes is one incident of being in the wrong place at the wrong time to ruin a life.

Once you have the right associates and friends in your inner circle, there are some realities African American youth must consider.

The rules of social engagement are different for people of color.

A black male walking down the street in a predominantly white community must accept the increased likelihood of being stopped and questioned by the police. The same applies to driving high-end luxury automobiles; you increase the odds of being pulled over when in exclusive or wealthy neighborhoods. It is important to always be conscious of our environment.

Another suggestion is to avoid walking into a retail establishment with a large posse or group of friends. Unfortunately, you will not get the benefit of the doubt that you're there to shop. It's assumed that large groups of minority youth congregating are up to no good. Swarming a retail establishment will increase the chances of being followed by store security. This may not seem fair but is a reality that our youth must learn to manage.

Interracial dating can be a touchy subject within African American homes. I share the opinion black people are some of the most forgiving and socially accepting people on the face of the earth.
An African American child's cultural socialization is seldom rooted in hate for other races, cultures and people. Our challenge comes with balancing the internal turmoil and memories of the historical treatment of blacks by other ethnic groups with our intrinsic moral conviction to forgive our oppressors. As recent as 1967, anti-miscegenation laws were enforced in America forbidding interracial marriage. Young black males have been killed for simply gazing at a white woman in the wrong way. Today's millennials are less inhibited concerning interracial dating.

In the end, it's understood you don't control who you love; but In America, who you love comes with consequences. Even today, interracial couples draw stares and remarks from perfect strangers who feel it's wrong to mix races and it is their responsibility to convey their displeasure. Interracial couples must be thick-skinned and committed to love and each other in order to survive.

ENGAGING LAW ENFORCEMENT:

The relationship between law enforcement and urban communities has been tenuous for some time. Allegations of abuse at the hands of police officers who are sworn to serve and protect its citizens date back to slavery and Jim Crow. Historically many of the elected officials and white leadership establishment were members of the KKK which compromised black folk's ability to trust many of those said to be in authority. It's also important to remember BLACK CODE LAW was enforced by law enforcement. I can remember conversations with older adults who acknowledged concern seeking assistance from local law enforcement for fear they may have encountered a dirty cop. The distrust of police has a long tradition among people of color, and this has always been a challenging subject for the reasons just mentioned.

Before I continue with this conversation about police and the African-American community, I think it's important that I clarify a few issues. There is a false assumption that black people do not want law and order in their neighborhoods. This is a ludicrous assumption. Black people, more than others have the most to gain if police honor their oath to serve and protect the communities assigned to them. The real issue is who can be trusted! Secondly, black communities need partnerships with the police not an occupying military that sees all young black men as potential criminals. Instead of creating a community policing presence where neighbors are allowed to get to know the police and build relationships, police, more often than not, assume the posture of an armed occupying force when engaging black communities. The tanks and military tactics demonstrated in Ferguson and Baltimore resembled troops on the ground in full combat. Which leads me to my last point, black folks do not assume all police officers are bad and are out to get them. As a young African American male, if the only interactions we have with the police are negative, violence will soon follow.

The practice of stopping and frisking as an example has led to disproportionate numbers of African American males implicated in America's criminal justice system. This law granted officers the authority to stop, pat down and search an individual based on their subjective profiling and suspicions a crime is about to be committed. Most concerning to me are the criteria used by Law Enforcement to profile a potential criminal. This is one way the media plays such a pervasive role in shaping public opinion. On a daily basis, when one turns on the evening news we subliminally receive a profile of what potential criminals look like:

1. African American males
2. Dreadlocks in hair
3. Wearing Hoody
4. Pants Sagging
5. Wears Nike or Adidas tennis shoes
6. Wears big gold chains

Are police using this profile to predict who might be more likely to commit a crime? Does this explain the disproportionate arrest of African American males? New York City adopted the stop and frisk policy as a part of their policing strategy. Statistics dating as far back as 2002 through 2015 suggest almost 88% of more than 4.4 million people stopped were innocent. Fewer than 12% of whites were pulled over. More than 30% of those stopped were Hispanics, and African-American males accounted for more than 51% of those stopped and questioned.

Profiling is another example of unequal justice in America's justice system. The activation results of the *Stop and Frisk* resembles just another form of BLACK CODE LAW. This profiling of African American males bothered me so much I decided to develop self-help and motivational speaking tour entitled "From the Bottom to the Top." Black men are featured in this seminar series who have overcome tremendous odds in transforming their lives from street cred to a life of significance. While it is good to acknowledge that unfair practices like *Stop and Frisk* exist it's more important that we provide solutions for young men to model in pursuit of their physical and emotional development into manhood. "From The Bottom To The Top Tour" is just such a tool.

For more information on the bottom to the top tour go to my website at www.fromthebottomtothetoptour.com.

Today the least of black male's worries is being stopped and frisked. The new more aggressive trend in urban communities across this nation is the shooting and murdering of unarmed black males suspected of having committed a crime. This practice not only devalues the lives of black men, it sharply highlights the two systems of justice being enforced in America. We must now ensure black males are taught the importance of deescalating highly emotionally charged environments. Following are five elements of "The Talk" focused on managing interactions with law enforcement.

1. Never Run:

When pulled over or stopped by the police you should never run. The likelihood you will escape is small and more importantly, if you have done nothing wrong don't risk being shot in the back or being roughed up when caught. Using the logic of risk versus reward, you must quickly access how to leverage this moment, so you arrive home safely.

2. Remain Calm, Cool & Collected:

I don't care who you are, when the blue lights of a police car are glaring in your rearview mirror your heart feels like it's going to jump out of your chest. The adrenaline rush is like none other. The ability to maintain composure when pulled over increases the odds of you safely surviving this encounter. No sudden hand movements and for God's sake do not get out of your car unless instructed by the officer.

3. Maintain A Respectful Tone of Voice:

Nothing escalates the risk of aggressive policing more than an irreverent tone in response to an officer's request. That does not mean you should surrender your rights as an American citizen. It only means being intentional about maintaining a tone that under normal conditions would earn you the respect you hope to receive. It is also important to be aware of our body language. More than 80% of communication is none verbal. Refusing to comply with simple directions or demonstrating aggressive gestures can escalate a police encounter as quickly as saying something that is condescending or off color. Remember the *Golden Rule*; do unto others as you would have them do unto you.

4. Know Your Rights:

I was amazed to discover that traffic violations are the #1 offense resulting in African Americans being entangled with the judicial system. Here's how it works:

- Your turn signal is not working
- Police pull you over
- You don't have current licenses and get arrested on the spot
- Your car is impounded and towed away because you cannot be allowed to drive without a valid driver's license.

The only way to avoid this encounter is to make sure you and the car you're driving both meet the essential requirements for you to safely and legally operate the vehicle. The point here is, try not to give police a reason to pull you over. Here's where this gets tricky when you're pulled over by an officer what would you do if faced with the following conditions. You're accused of driving erratic, and that's why the police pulled you over. The officer requests permission to inspect your car or worse yet opens your driver side rear door and begins to search the vehicle. What you say or do next is important. Remember; stay calm, cool and collected.

Ensure your tone and voice inflection are appropriate and respectful when you ask the officer the following question: "Officer, do you have a warrant to inspect my car? Without a warrant, I respectfully decline the search of my vehicle." When sharing this strategy, I have had some to disagree, concerned that refusing the search if you have nothing to hide only provides the police greater cause to suspect you of having done wrong. As an American citizen, our judicial system says we are innocent until proven guilty. You would be surprised to know how many victims fall prey to an illegal search of their vehicles. When the search is approved, and illegal contraband is found, it will inevitably be tied to the owner of or driver of the vehicle. You avoid this possibility when you decline an illegal search of your transportation.

Another incident youth should be aware of is when to ask a police officer if you are being detained. The point here is a police has the right to pull you over and state the reason for pulling you over. When questioning transitions from general to specific inquiries you have the right to ask the officer are you being detained. If the officer says yes, ask the officer to please explain the charges. If not, please request to be released. The key to this entire exchange is to know your rights but recognize the importance of delivering objections in a respectful manner. This is not the time or place to demonstrate your street swagger. Talking loud and making assertive demands will only infuriate the officer. Never back an officer in a corner or push him/her to the limits of their patience. As a young African American male, you must never forget the desired end game is to get out of this situation alive!

5. Never Threaten An Officer:

In recent years, *Stand Your Ground Laws* have been passed that empowers police and regular citizens with the right to protect themselves when it can be proven a deadly physical threat exist. The vagueness of this CODE LAW clearly provides law enforcement justification for taking offensive measures that may end in taking the life of an assailant if he/she fears for their life. This single law has become a game changer with respect to its impact on the African-American community.

Trayvon Martin's murder in Sanford, Florida crystalized the subversive institutionalized nature of racism in America. Here we had a neighborhood watch captain using the *Stand Your Ground Law* in defense of killing an unarmed 17-year old black male walking through his father's gated community at night. This murder polarized the country and led to one of the most racially divisive incidents in this nation's history.

Trayvon Martin, who was staying with his father over the summer, was profiled and followed by a neighborhood watchman who felt Trayvon was up to no good and confronted him. The evidence suggests the two exchanged blows and at some point during this altercation; an armed George Zimmerman supposedly felt threatened, drew his firearm and shot a 17- year -old unarmed child in the chest and murdered him.

This case was of particular significance to me because I grew up in East Saint Louis Illinois, as did Tracy Martin, Trayvon's father. Two years after this Trayvon's murder I had an opportunity to reunite with Tracy Martin and was privileged to interview him on matters relative to this case. I was somewhat surprised to witness the throngs of people who came out to hear what Tracy had to say two years after the incident. The turnout served as proof the case touched the lives of millions of African American families coupled with a sense of pride in how Tracy and Sabrina Fulton, Trayvon's parents, handled themselves under the spotlight of such a tragedy. Tracy explained as a parent, he had administered "The Talk," enrolled Trayvon in youth leadership programs in the community and had a good relationship with his son.

Trayvon had structure and people who loved and cared for him in his life; yet, he fell victim to being profiled when he had every right to be in the Sanford gated community as anyone else who lived there. Why would a hoody make him so sinister that George Zimmerman would suspect he was up to no good? In recent years; the trust gap between urban communities and police has widened. Black men have often felt they have a target on their backs. The following chart highlights several of the more heavily publicized murders of unarmed black youth at the hands of law enforcement.

John Crowford	2014	Ohio	Playing with air riffle display in Wal Mart
Eric Garner	2014	NY	Selling cigarettes on the street corner
Michael Brown	2014	Missouri	Walking in the streets unarmed
Ezell Ford	2014	California	Unarmed during an investigative stop
Jordan Davis	2013	Florida	Playing music too loud
Travon Martin	2012	Florida	Walking in the wrong neighborhood with hoody on
Oscar Grant	2009	California	Unarmed cuffed and on his stomic was still shoot
Sean Bell	2006	NY	Wrong place wrong time
Amadour Diallo	1999	NY	Fourty one shoots fired into an unarmed man

RECENT UNARMED AFRICAN AMERICAN MALE MURDER VICTIMS AT THE HANDS OF LAW ENFORCEMENT

THE CODE

In recent years I have witnessed such unrest in the African American community surrounding the devaluing of the lives of African American males. Not since the murder of Emmett Till, a 14-year-old African-American young man murdered in August of 1955 in Mississippi for allegedly whistling at a white woman, have there been such a public outcry for justice. All the while the list of victims seems to continue to grow daily. No sooner than one crisis cools down and the protests subside, another African American male is being gunned down on the streets of urban cities across this country.

Homegrown terrorist are assaulting the black community disguised as law enforcement supposedly bound and sworn to protect African American citizens. As I'm writing this chapter, two critical cases are in the process of working themselves through the courts. Recently, Laquan McDonald, a 17-year-old Chicago youth was shot 16 times within 15 seconds. Dash cam video evidence confirms 13 of the 15 seconds the victim was already on the ground. In this case, the police lied in the original report claiming Laquan was aggressively coming toward them when they opened fire in defense of their lives. For almost a year the police refused to release the video cam evidence until a state judge demanded the release of the tape. The video contradicted the facts presented by the police and pointed to a major cover-up attempt to suppress the fact that Laquan was murdered by police officer Jason Van Dyke.

The same day the video was released the local prosecutor charged the officer with the assassination of Laquan McDonald. Then there is the case of Freddie Gray. Mr. Gray, a 25-year-old African American male from Baltimore, Maryland was murdered after being arrested for possessing a switchblade knife. In the process of being transported to the police station, Mr. Gray was subjected to what is referred to as a rough ride in the rear of the police van. Mr. Gray's fatal injuries included three fractured vertebrae, injuries to his voice box, and his spine was 80% severed at his neck. The first of six police officers charged in Mr. Gray's murder trial ended in a hung jury. After weeks of unrest and riots for justice, the first of Mr. Gray's murders walked out of the courthouse a free man.

What frustrates me most is the senseless nature of the violence that's ending the lives of black males. There appears to be a shoot first and ask a question later mentality among police in urban neighborhoods that is unacceptable and would not be tolerated in white advantaged communities. Help me understand how on November 20, 2015, a white man could enter into an Apple store on 5th Avenue New York, full of customers, swinging a sword and New York police show restraint in subduing and arresting him without cause for a fatal incident.

Yet, eight months earlier an Air Force veteran Anthony Hill, suffering from mental issues, running necked through his DeKalb County, GA neighborhood is murdered by a police who claims he felt threatened by Mr. Hill, who was unarmed at the time of the incident.

Take for instance the shooting of 18-year-old African American male, Michael Brown, of Ferguson, Missouri. Michael Brown and a friend were walking in the streets when they were confronted by Officer Darion Wilson. Evidence suggests words were exchanged, and a struggle ensued leading to Mr. Brown running away from the police car in attempt to flee the scene. Witnesses testified that as Mr. Brown was running away from Officer Wilson when the police officer stepped out of his vehicle and fired his revolver hitting the subject more than six times. The lethal shot allegedly occurred as Mr. Brown was facing the officer and going to his knees holding his hands up as a sign of surrender. As far as we know, the only infraction the police suspected Mr. Brown of being guilty of at the time of the incident was walking in the middle of the street. How did such an incident escalate to the gunning down of an unarmed 18-year old teenager on the streets of a Ferguson neighborhood?

This case went before a grand jury and no charges were filed. Former Officer Wilson got off free. Another example of excessive force in urban communities is the John Crawford case. When did it become illegal for a customer, shopping in a Wal-Mart, admiring an air rifle on display being sold in the store's sporting goods section be shot dead on the spot? John Crawford was shot in cold blood with his last words being "It's not real." What was it about Mr. Crawford that caused law enforcement to assume the worse and convince them this young black man was up to no good? Why was there no apparent restraint on the part of the two officers that gunned down Mr. Crawford? Didn't they recognize they were in a retail sporting goods store environment that happens to sell the same make and model BB gun the gentlemen was holding?

When did selling single cigarettes on the street corners of America's cities become a capital offense punishable by death? Who authorized the officer to ignore the cries of Mr. Eric Garner, who screamed out more than eleven times he could not breathe as the officer applied an illegal choke hold on him?

What kind of world are we living in when 17- year -old Jordan Davis was killed for playing his music too loud in Jacksonville, Florida? Yea, I'm sure words were exchanged between Mr. Jordan and the man who murdered him but how do you justify shooting eight times into a car of unarmed teens?

The streets of Ferguson Missouri, Queens Staten, Island NY, Jacksonville Florida and Sanford Florida among others are raging in hopes that justice will prevail. I'm sure I am not alone in wondering why the police officers are so afraid. They're the ones with guns and the authority to legally kill. Something has gone terribly wrong when corrupt police officers, who are paid to protect and empower the communities they are assigned to serve, are shooting young black men dead in the streets in alarming numbers, and increasing frequency and we remain silent as a community!

More than 170 unarmed African American males were shot and killed by law enforcement in 2015 alone. Legislation to require officers to wear body cam represents a step in the right direction but as a community we must use our collective voices to demand more of our public servants!

It's also critical that a part of our responsibility as parents, mentors and community leaders is to educate our youth on how to interact socially in a hostile world. We must continue to "Talk" to our youth and share the values and behaviors that have enabled the black community to preserver in the face of some difficult times.

Last but clearly not least, we as a black community must not sink so low as to charge all law enforcement officers with being corrupt. I am reminded of the recent loss of Riverdale Police Maj. Greg Barney who was killed assisting in performing a warrant arrest of a local suspected drug dealer when he lost his life. What a legacy of service he left with members of the community he serviced acknowledging his efforts to mentor and care for the youth in the city he was sworn to serve. We must challenge the system to rid themselves of bad cops and the leaders and institutional racist policies that stoke the current flames of suspicion in black communities.

THE CODE GUIDE:

- The "TALK" is a part of the rites of passage for African American youth
- Black males are at greater risk of losing their lives at the hands of a police officer or another black man
- Teaching and equipping our youth with strategies to de-escalate highly emotionally charged encounters is our responsibility as parents, mentors and surrogate fathers
- Socializing our young people to what they may confront at the hands of racist is critical
- We must never forget everything that is legal is not just.
- Teaching our youth to recognize and navigate the injustices they will face because of the color of their skin increases the odds they will make it home safe each night
- The community must play a role in protecting our youth

Chapter 7

The black family survived centuries of slavery and generations of Jim Crow, but it has disintegrated in the wake of the liberals' expansion of the welfare state.

Thomas Sowell

FATHERLESS COMMUNITIES

What in the world happen to the black family? Growing up, one of my favorite television shows was Good Times. James Evans represented black America's blue-collar father. James was always looking for an opportunity to lift his family from poverty. His strong work ethic was admirable, and he always seemed to have a hustle on the side to help make ends meet. Florida was both a loving wife and mother who recognized her husband's flaws and his strengths.

She was his ride and die chick that supported her man and made sure she honored and respected his role as head of house without feeling threatened or compromised in her role. James Jr. or J.J. Thelma and Michael were well-mannered children who seldom got into serious trouble but each in their unique way provided a platform for the issues black youth are forced to deal with growing up in the hood. The Evans family lived in the Chicago housing projects. While considered poor; they were rich in the love and friendships they shared within their community. The Evans family was far from being the Cosby Show Huxtable family with Cliff and Claire a doctor and attorney by trade. However, the Evans family was every bit as important. Even George and Louise Jefferson of The Jefferson's demonstrated the importance of family in our community.

Today we have The Atlanta Housewives where more of the main characters are single than those married. Then there are the Braxton's. While Vince and Tamar represent the institution of marriage, the Braxton matriarch, and other Braxton sisters appear far less traditional in how they practice their marital vowels. Today with the demand for reality TV shows, very few shows depict balanced African American family life inclusive of both a father and mother as core characters. If you're like me, you're wondering where have the black families gone? America is now 56 years removed from President Lyndon B. Johnson's War On Poverty legislation which in 1960 was created to reduce the number of families living beneath the poverty level in America. At the time, more than 22% of American citizens were living beneath the poverty line. On the surface, the war on poverty would appear to be a good social policy for all. As it turns out, it was good for everyone except black fathers and the black family.

America's social welfare legislative policies disintegrated black family values. In only 56 years The War on Poverty set the black family back more so than the preceding 286 years of slavery. While the media takes great pleasure in pointing out how many absentee fathers there are in the black community, few take the time to share how we arrived at this place in time. There was a day when the black family was the strength and the backbone that held our communities together.

The institution of slavery couldn't destroy the institution of marriage and co-dependence on each other in the black community. Yea, there were slaves who were allowed to marry formally by their masters. Many state laws deemed it illegal to marry as slaves, but that didn't stop families from forming among the African slaves. Some plantation owners refused to allow slaves to marry due to the practice of selling off slaves, and the plantation owners didn't want to grapple with splitting married families. Plantation owners also wanted to have their way with slave women when they wanted. Based on census data and surveying of once slaves who lived after the 1865 post-Emancipation of slaves period, more than 51% of slave families consisted of two-parent households with both a father and mother present in the same living quarters on the same plantation. Approximately 12.4% of slave families maintained a unit but were forced to adjust to living on a plantation that allowed frequent visitation.

Thirty-one percent of slave families were female-headed households. Between 15-20% of those accounted as the single female-headed households were from children birthed with the female slaves white masters. In spite of the fact, families were sold and separated from each other; marriage remained a viable and valued institution during and immediately after slavery.

Even after the abolishing of slavery, fewer than 2% of slave families voluntarily divorced. More than 80% of slave families sold off and separated by slavery were reunited after slavery. Even after death, fewer than 2% of slave wives remarried. During the 1960 civil rights period, 80% of black households were two-parent homes consisting of a father, mother, and children. Something radical occurred between 1960 and 1985. Black single parent female headed household increased from 20.6% to 43.7%. During this same period, white single female-headed households rose from 8.4 to 12%. Today more than 77% of newborn African-American children live in single female headed households. Compare that to whites to whom 74% of children are born into two-parent households and 83% of Asians. The question is what's going on with the black family?

First, as cited earlier, history dispels the notion black men don't love or care for their children. I get worked up when I read articles and see news reports that call into question the morals of black people without placing in context our 286 years of slavery in America. Our people were forcefully chained to the bottom of slave ships, separating fathers, mothers, sisters and brothers and sold into slavery. Right Wing politicians have the nerve to condemn black folk for our moral decay and lack of family values. Where do you think we learned such behavior? Suffice it to say, that much of the way we turned out originates from our 286 years of on-the-job training received from our slave masters.

During this period, a massive number of citizens migrated from the south to major urban cities in search of a better quality of life. Manufacturing jobs were in plentiful supply, and many of the Southern blacks who had been trying to scratch out a living sharecropping on small farms were a part of this massive move to the cities. Urban housing was built to accommodate the migration to largely black populated communities which sprung up in Detroit, Chicago, Saint Louis, Ohio and other larger cities.

Again manufacturing and eventually service jobs were concentrated in these cities. While they did pay more than those they left in the south, they were still overwhelmingly low paying jobs. It is worth mentioning from 1939 -1945 America was embroiled in World War II. A workforce revolution occurred during this period. When men were drafted to fight in the war, women replaced them working jobs left idle in their absence. The feminist movement which started in 1960-1970 was the next social phenomena to impact American culture. The feminist movement was birthed out of a desire promote gender equality. It was not by coincidence that between 1959 and 1968 there was a 54% reduction in the number of households headed by African American males 65 years of age or less. During the same period, female-headed households increased from 30 to 43%. Sadly black female-headed households disproportionally accounted for greater than 80% of families needing welfare support. The real question is what changed within the black community resulting in an increase in single female-headed households? **Black women experienced a shift in their values and beliefs and abandoned the notion of getting married during early age.** In 1960 black woman married at almost the same rate as white women. Today the majority of black woman are delaying marriage but continue to have babies at a rate of approximately 80% out of wedlock.

For a moment, I want you to reflect back on the lessons learned from chapter 4. The plantation owner sought to dismantle the black male by altering the natural order of the black family. The natural order consisted of the traditional married, two-parent household with children. If the black families had continued the traditional path of supporting their children in a two-parent home, the poverty level would be different. Statistics suggest that fewer than 2% of black families with two parents live in poverty. Conversely single female-headed households now account for more than 80% of the children who live in poverty. It should be noted; this percent continues to climb! It is not my intent to offend anyone, but let me be clear; having children out of wedlock without the financial and emotional means of raising them has destroyed the African American community.

When I hear young ladies talking about becoming "BOSSES" and running things and how they "don't need a man," I swear; I just want to throw up! Two critical points I need to make here:

1) I believe in the value of a welfare safety net
2) I am an advocate for women fulfilling their potential.

When I was young, I remember receiving food stamps. I've benefited from government cheese and those large cans of peanut butter with the oil on the top. As a child, I remember eating spam meat and felt grateful there was the support to help my parents when they needed it most. I shared earlier; one of my favorite TV shows was Good Times. James Evans, the lead character for those of you that know anything about the show, was unemployed more than employed on the show. What I loved about James was he was a proud black man! James always had a hustle on the side. From repairing electronics to working day construction jobs, you seldom saw him just sitting around. He didn't want charity or pity from anyone and would not accept it! What he wanted was a job or hand-up, not a handout.

Somewhere along the way we bought into the slave master's diabolical plan. Black babies started having children of their own, willing to accept sex over waiting for someone who would love and marry them before taking on the role of parent. Then we discovered there was a welfare system that would compensate us for our moral lapse in judgment. We also bought into the fact we received more welfare money when we had more children. Many mistakenly saw the social welfare system not as an emergency recovery system but as a way of life. With no incentive to go out and get a job, just like the slave masters predicted, the woman trained her daughters to duplicate her life choices and head up the household while moms coddled their black sons, allowing him to advance on the levels on PlayStation gaming; instead of advancing in their career prospects. Far too many moms have raised their sons to be physically fit but emotionally weak. He fills entitled and has a hair-thin temper and zero ambition; a formula for disaster!

Then the War on Poverty struck the most lethal blow to the black community. Welfare incentives were structured so as to penalize two parent house and common law relationships by reducing the payout when a black male was present in the home. Men, many of us moved or pretended not to live in the same household as our family. We played the game and look at what has occurred with the dynamics of the black family. Slave-master got us just where he wanted us.

Secondly, I have always supported a woman's right to independently use her gifts to flourish in life. On the other hand as a man, I have also sought to make the woman in my life feel comfortable. Most good men want to provide and protect those he loves. I am no different, given the choice; I would rather run through hell dipped in gasoline, so my wife and son are not forced to do something solely for the sake of taking care of our household. That's just the values I was raised with. That is my responsibility as a man! That's just me! This is not a right or wrong issue. I relish in my traditional role of being a provider. I think some women have taken this new BOSS Phenom too far. It bothers me to hear women say "I don't need a man." This quest for independence has driven a wedge between black couples. A good man wants to open his lady's or his wife's door when getting in the car or entering their home. When a woman tells a man there is no need for his services; she destroys him. Just like the horses were used to pull his body apart, you kill his spirit. Now because you have trained him as such, he only seeks you out when he wants sex. Men are not looking for a BOSS. A good man is looking for a wife with the potential to be a great mother of his children.

THE CODE GUIDE:

- The black family had always been the strongest institution in our community
- Our faith has always been our guide and influenced our values and morals
- Slavery didn't break up the black family
- Social welfare and a change in our values destroyed the black family
- Female-headed households outnumber male-headed households in the black community
- The BOSS complex is destroying the African-American community
- Black males need to step up and assume the role of leader in their family

Chapter 8

I was an aspiring astrophysicist, and that's how I defined myself, not by my skin color. People didn't treat me as someone with science ambitions. They treated me as someone they thought was going to mug them, or who was a shoplifter.

Neil deGrasse Tyson

TRANSFORMING THE IMAGE OF BLACK MEN

Growing up and transitioning through those very challenging teenage years, I can remember times when I stood in the mirror and picked myself apart. Every flaw stood out to me. Everything I didn't like and wished I didn't have screamed my name.

I now recognize my critique was unfair. What was my comparison? That darned 1979 poster of the artist known as Prince with no shirt. The young ladies in my 8th-grade class at Lansdowne Jr. High school Ernestine Daniels, Schneil Dunn Yolanda Manning were going crazy over him. What must it feel like, I wondered, to look like Prince? The real issue was I didn't like who I was. Most black men in America, if we are honest, have had the experience of looking ourselves in the mirror and picking ourselves apart. Black men are the target of ridicule. Society and local media provide the black man a laundry list of glaring reminders that we are not perfect. We rank among the highest in dropout rates, the lowest percent employed. The negative images associated with being a black man at first glance appear overwhelming! If you haven't figured it out by now the conspiracy to criminalize the black male in America and all around the world has been tied to strategic plans to destroy our image and ultimately our spirt. The goal has been to break us! Now more than ever before its time for black men to lift our voices and reestablish the rule and order of the Kingdom!

Because we are lone wolves, we often cry and die in silent isolation. Like robots, we have been programmed to show no empathy and human emotion. When lost in life's storms, rather than ask for help we choose death, deeming it more honorable. We have been conditioned to believe letting someone into our deepest thoughts, and emotions make us vulnerable, and somehow less than a man. There are few things worse in life, including death than for a man allowing himself to feel venerable to someone else. We relish in the fact that on the surface, all seems well when deep inside we're crying and dying way too soon. If we are to transform our image, we must take an active role in positioning ourselves to receive that which empowers us to be great. What most black men live for and are willing to die for are three simple things:

1. Respect
2. Recognition
3. Reward

RESPECT:

Since the origins of black men in America, he has been the target of disrespect. There is a hole in every black man's heart craving to be respected. Slavery conditioned black men to tolerate disrespect as a natural state of life. Slavery was a learned behavior. It's not natural for a man to take being abused and disrespected. When the slave master called him out of his name and beat him within an inch of his life, he refused to scream out for mercy. Stripped naked of both his clothing and dignity knowing his wife and children were watching, he learned to fight with the weapons he possessed within himself. His defiance in not screaming out in pain when lashed by suppressing the pain has contributed to the pent-up rage in black men today. This is in part why I believe we are willing to kill each other over the slightest offense refusing to be disrespected! When the slave master's whip us our refusal to cry out represented our silent protest to being disrespected. When the plantation owner came to his slave house and forcefully took his wife and had his way with her, restraint was his only recourse in protest of his demand to be respected. Respect says I recognize your value and affirm the fact you matter. In order to transform the image of black men, we must commit ourselves to aligning our works with vales that will reestablish respectability in the African American community.

RECOGNITION:

Men are warriors at heart. Competing is a part of our DNA. When challenged he will fight. The goal of any challenge is to win. The way to motivate most men is to praise them for what they do well or to challenge them by telling him what he cannot do. When told what he cannot achieve, a man will attempt to prove you wrong ever time. This deep seeded desire for recognition is a part of his personality. Mothers when you give your sons everything they want, and never demand anything of him, you kill the hunter in him! A problem requires a man to be resourceful in figuring out a solution. He will give his all to achieve what is important to him, and nothing can impede a passionate man who knows what and why he was purposed to do a thing.

REWARD

A $10.00 bill is worth $10.00 even if crumble and tossed to the ground; the value of the currency remains undiminished. The reality is so many black men when compared to their Caucasian peers are made to feel inferior. Black men are required to endure the opinion of the critics and persevere in spite of opposition. The key to affirming a black man's efforts is to reward him for his achievements. Real men will not linger where not appreciated.

I will close this section and this chapter with a story about a guy who was selling his talking dog. He placed a sign in the front yard that said "Talking Dog for Sale." It wasn't too long after he put the sign in his front yard that a couple who were out walking in the neighborhood saw the sign and said to each other how interesting, let's take a look. The couple rang the doorbell, and the owner opened the door with a big smile on his face asking how he could help. The couple and owner exchanged greetings, and when it was clarified they were interested in the dog, the owner suggested they see the dog in the backyard.

Sure enough, when they walked in the back yard, the dog stood at attention and clear as a bell said to the couple, "How are you doing? I'm Sam, the talking dog." The couple looked at each other in amazement. You really can talk; they said in unison! Sam went on for about ten minutes sharing with them how he had once been a spy for the CIA and even worked in the White House for a period sitting at the feet of the President while he was in foreign negotiations with Russia. No one ever suspected the dog to understand and interpret Russian for the government. The conversation soon tailed off, and they bid Sam the dog farewell and returned to the main house.

The owner met them at the door. "What do you think?" He is great. How much are you asking for him, the couple asked? I'll take $20.00. The couple looked at each other in utter amazement. Twenty dollars! Sir, why would you be willing to sell Sam for so little? Oh, he must have told you the story about the CIA and his time in the White House. Well, you should know, Sam is nothing but a liar. The dog has never been out of that back yard!

While this may be funny to those, who got the punch line the circumstances play out on the streets every day. The owner attributed no value to the fact he owned the most intelligent and only speaking dog in the entire world. For this owner, he only valued what he deemed to be truth and integrity. If we are to demand the world respect black men, black men we must begin to value our own lives. To know that people are waiting on side streets and small towns under less than privileged conditions, waiting to hear your voice should encourage you. Your voice is the only one that will quench the thirst and heal the wounds tied to someone's suffering. You and only you are the solutions to someone's problem. And to think you've been walking around comparing yourself to someone else and critiquing and highlighting every flaw and fragile place in your life. Look into that mirror again and tell me what you see. I see the King in you.

THE CODE GUIDE:

- Self-worth is inherent in all humanity
- When you compare yourself to idols, you will always come up short
- Surround yourself with people who hear your voice and see your vision
- If you are the smartest person in your circle of friends, know you need to find some new friends if you want to grow
- Recognize your value even if no one else does

Chapter 9

I'm stronger because I had to be. I'm smarter because of my mistakes. I'm happier because of the sadness I've known. NOW I am wiser because I learned.
Unknown

THE HEART AND SOUL OF A BLACK MAN

Over the years, I've gained the reputation of being the assemblyman. You know, the person who can remove the bicycle or office furniture from the box and with a little time invested, assemble the project. The ability to construct items has been a useful skill over the years.

I doubt I'll ever win any awards for this gift, but the capacity to pull together separate and distinct pieces and assemble them, so they fit and work in harmony with each other is a great skill to carry out into the world as it relates to interacting with people.

It's funny; I remember when I wasn't so good at assembling things. Like many people, there was a time in my life I would rip open the box and based on my logic, try to construct the item. Time and time again I found myself investing hours and days in my attempt to figure out how to assemble the project before I had to scrap it all and start again from scratch. It was not until I learned to lean on the insights and instructions included in the manufactures guide that my skill set began to improve in this area. The manufacturers guide is the greatest source of guidance when diagnosing a problem. All my life has been spent trying to assemble myself into the perfect gentlemen. I was fortunate enough to acquire a secondary and post-secondary education, but none of my formal academic training prepared me with the skills and knowledge to be a successful black man in America.

For years, I stumbled in the darkness trying to assemble myself; trying to adjoin the awkwardly shaped pieces. I was in search of balance, harmony, and peace. At a point in my life, I had to face the fact that what I had created was a life filled with a succession of failures, setbacks, disappointments and stress. America's conspiracy against black males is to convince us we are failures. I was playing right into the hands of the conspiracy to destroy black males.

When talking to other men, I realized I was not alone. I discovered many African American men needed a blueprint to guide their lives. Let me explain. Growing up I watched my mother, a pretty good seamstress in her own rights, make outfits. Back in the day, they were referred to as homemade clothes. To achieve this, I remember us going to local linen shops where they sold patterns. I remember comparing the photos of what the finished item would look like to determine which outfit I liked best. For the cost of a $1 pattern and a $10 bolt of material, my mother could make anything.

THE CODE

This book was designed to be a blueprint and a resource guide to aid in navigating the many obstacles that have been thrown in the path of black men to impede our progress. The title of this book "THE CODE" is symbolic of social and political forces within this country and around the world that are working together in a conspiracy to demoralize and ultimately criminalize the image of black men.
BLACK CODES were legally enforceable racist legislative state policies designed to derail the progress of former slaves.
Today black men continue to face opposition and distrust birthed from racist origins that have been institutionalized into America's cultural norms.

The "The War on Drugs" and "The War on Poverty" were both legally adopted social policies that contributed to the demise of the black family. The miseducation of African American males is another civil rights crisis we must address! We cannot afford to have 53% of young African American men not to receive a high school diploma. Lastly, the criminalization of African American men and the expansion of the Prison Industrial Complex have made incarcerating black males profitable. Black men are disproportionately criminalized and exploited for their free labor within the prison system. This practice must stop!

The criminal justice system must become a just system for all of America's citizens.

.

THE SOLUTION:

Well, I would be remiss if didn't share with you what helped be align my life after spending so many years trying to fix myself.

Brothers, you need to know the author of the original manufacturers' manual is our Heavenly Father. It's written in the bestselling book of all time, the Bible. Not the slave masters textbook, not our oppressor's religion but the wisdom from the source of all living things, GOD, the Creator. There are principles in this book that defy the test of time and human logic. Simple truths, when we embrace them and live by them, will empower us to flourish in life.

The first principle is to discover your PURPOSE.

IDENTIFY THE PURPOSE FOR YOUR LIFE:

The Bible speaks of the creation of the first man Adam. The Bible says God created Adam from the dust of the ground.

Adam's significance came from his creator. Brothers no matter how long you look you will only find significance and purpose in life within God's blueprint for your life. Money won't do it. Rich men die lonely and empty lives every day with more money than they were able to spend in a lifetime. Fame will not do it. The fact that the world knows your name will not extend your life by one second.

Fulfillment, peace and joy come when you understand and are in active pursuit of the particular reason God allowed you to be birthed into the world. What the conspirators meant for evil, God can and will use for your good. Brothers get to know your creator. Ask for help. He knows how you feel and what you're going through and will be there for you during life's most difficult moments.

DISCOVER YOUR PLACE:

Principle two; you will flourish when you discover the environment designed to help you maximize your potential. Adam was created from the dust within a wild and desolate place. God then took the man he created and placed him in a beautiful oasis garden brimming over with every species of fruit and vegetation known. The garden was also occupied by every animal to walk the earth. The garden provided for all of Adams needs.

Adam's greatest preference in life was working with plants and animals. The Creator recognizing Adams talents and what he took pleasure in and assigned him the responsibility of tending to the garden and naming every animal in the garden. Adam was the world's first horticulturist for his love of working with plant and the world's first zoologist for his passion for working with animals. Adam was successful because he was in the right place.

STOP TRYING TO DO IT YOUR WAY:

I stumbled around for years trying to find the place I belonged. For years, I tried directing my destiny. Working in corporate America, I moved more than 12 times in 24 years. I was chasing success and felt uprooting my family from city to city, town to town was the solution to the burning desire I had to prove the world wrong and to achieve success in America as a black man. God used my son to adjust my thinking. When I moved my family from Jacksonville, Florida to Atlanta Georgia back in 2007 I credited God with ordering my steps. I had always wanted to live in Atlanta, the chocolate city of success and opportunity for black folks in the south. My son was approximately 12-years old at the time. After residing in Atlanta six months or so my wife and I noticed our son was not making friends easy.

We assumed it would pass. When it didn't, I pressed him to explain why? Silence was his response to my inquiry. I persisted, and then he said it; "I'm tired of making two-year friends." At first, it went right over my head. Then like a bolt of lightning, it hit me. My son was telling me he was tired of making friends he was able to only nurture for two years or less before we moved again. Ouch! Not only had I let my son down but had placed my wife under unnecessary stress and strain chasing my dream of success all around the country. How selfish I had been. Through all my trials I came to recognize the only place of safety, security and succcsscs was in God's plan for my life. See I can't truly say I ever sought God's direction in any of my moves. I thought I controlled my destiny. I'm am still a work in progress, but I now recognize the greatest moments of success had been when I trusted God to order my steps and obeyed His leading.

IDENTIFY WHO YOU WERE CREATED TO SERVE:

Last it is critical that you identify those things you have a passion for and the people you were created to serve. As stated earlier, Adam enjoyed working with animals and plants. Because the creator knew he was good at it and that he enjoyed it, so that became his job. Every man needs a job. A job gives a man purpose.

Don't just settle for a job, look to secure the work you were created to fulfill. Your work will be connected to serving others with your gifts and talents. The journey of life is discovering the service and people we are to commit ourselves. I have always had a passion to encourage and inspire the underdog. Individuals who have the potential but lack the confidence and direction to succeed in life. I have a passion for seeing black men stand up and be counted as the leaders and models of success we are. Tied up in Adam's job assignment was his responsibility to protect and to cultivate the animals and the vegetation in the garden. Within every man is a burning desire to protect those he loves. When Eve, Adams wife and his children were born, his responsibility extended to protect those assigned to his care. As a man, your desire to protect your family should come naturally.

Real men take pride in providing for their loved ones. The sure sign you have transitioned from being a boy to a man is when you willingly sacrifice of yourself for those you love. Boys will always think to take care of their selfish needs and wants first. Men recognize the responsibility to serve and provide for those he loves. When I began to align my life with these simple principles, my life started to flourish. Thank you for taking this journey with me. I hope you are better equipped to crack the CODES and open the bank vaults to the love, peace and wealth you desire.

THE CODE GUIDE:

- It's difficult on our own to become a good man
- We need models and people who inspire us to help us
- Being lost is a part of the journey so don't be discouraged
- Find someone who has achieved what you desire to become
- Ask questions and request their support in mentoring you
- The real significance of life is the service you can provide to others
- Learn to be patient
- Discover your purpose for living
- Seek the wisdom of your creator
- Look to connect with those people who hear your voice
- Serve others and life will serve you

ABOUT THE AUTHOR

Cornelius Stafford is a dynamic speaker and author blessed with a unique gift to touch the hearts of the lost, hurting and forgotten of society. His messages will challenge and inspire you to fulfill your potential.

Mr. Stafford was born in East Saint Louis, Illinois, recognized among America's poorest cities. His life stands as a testament to the resilience of the human spirit in overcoming tremendous odds. The death of his parents at an early age, the experiences of growing up in the housing projects of East Saint Louis, and his struggles with identity/self-esteem and his personal health challenges are all a part of his resume. It is from this sorted past that Mr. Stafford credits for having provided him his greatest source of inspiration.

Mr. Stafford's passion is helping individuals and organizations to identify, develop and reach their full potential. As an author and professional speaker, Mr. Stafford enjoys empowering people by providing them with information and resources that enable them to lead more productive lives. One way that Mr. Stafford makes a difference is by sharing his messages of hope through his professional training company, CS Inspires. Mr. Stafford is the author of The M.I.A. Crisis, a CD project that focuses attention on the alarming number of men missing in action from their homes, churches and communities. He is also the author of "Pathway To Purpose a story of overcoming life's challenges and winning!

Mr. Stafford was the former President of 100 Black Men of DeKalb County, Inc. Mr. Stafford was the 2013 Mentor of the Year for the 100 Black Men of America, Inc., an international community service organization with more than 10,000 members and 114 chapters worldwide.

Mr. Stafford is also a health care advocate through his national awareness campaign called "Black To Life" focusing attention on alarming crisis surrounding organ failure and the need for registered donors in the African American community. Cornelius Stafford is also a member of Alpha Phi Alpha Fraternity. Mr. Stafford's lovely wife of twenty-five years is Mrs. Patricia Stafford. They have one son, Cortlyn Jimmel Stafford. They reside in metro Atlanta, Georgia.

Need A Speaker?

Author and motivational speaker, Mr. Cornelius Stafford is one of the most inspiring and empowering speakers on the circuit.
His more than 25-year career as a manager an industry professional at Fortune 100 automotive giant, Chrysler Group, LLC affords him the ability to speak on a broad range of business topics. As an Operations Manager with the likes of Chrysler and State Farm, Mr. Stafford has a vast knowledge of the strategies and techniques that separate the most profitable industry leaders from average and subpar performers. Mr. Stafford expertise is the area of process and personnel management. Looking for someone to help you boost profits, reduce employee turnover and increase customer retention and average gross sales per transaction, Cornelius Stafford is your guy.

As a community activist, Mr. Stafford has assembled an impressive resume of accomplishments. Mr. Stafford is a former distinguished winner of the 100 Black Men of America's Mentor of The Year Award, where he was selected from its more than ten thousand members and 114 chapters worldwide! Mr. Stafford also formally served as the president and chief operating officer of the 100 Black Men of DeKalb County chapter. Contact Mr. Stafford's through his website at:www.thecodemyvirtualmentor.com

Office phone at 1-866-686-5836 or email at; csinspires@aol.com

Speaking Topics Include, But Are Not Limited To The Following Subjects:

- The Power In Servant Leadership
- How To Transform Your Career
- Discovering Your Purpose
- Overcoming Challenging Times
- Developing Inspired Employees
- Do you Understand Your Value
- Mentoring African American Boys
- How To Increase Customer Retention

Consider booking Mr. Stafford for your next event.

Cornelius Stafford CS Inspires Inc.
1-866-686-5836
wwwthecodemyvirtualmentor.com

THE M.I.A. CRISIS

A PROGRAM DEDICATED TO MEN MENTORING MEN

PATHWAY TO PURPOSE

ONE MAN'S JOURNEY IN TRANSFORMING LIFE'S CHALLENGES TO LIFE'S TRIUMPHS

NEED A MENTOR IN YOUR LIFE?

TEXT THE WORD 1MENTOR TO 97000

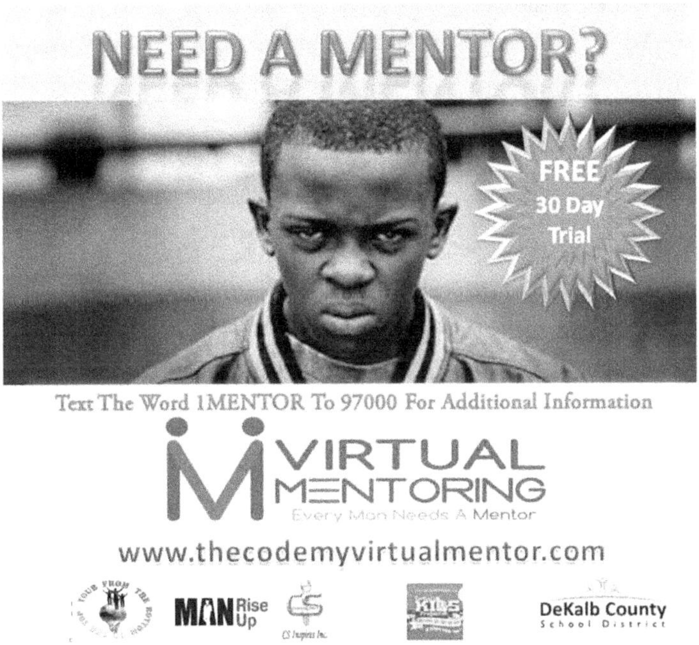

Final Notes and Reference

Related links:

- Wikiquote,:https://en.wikiquote.org/wiki/Sun_Tzu
- legal-dictionary.thefreedictionary.com/vagrancy
- Historical Document: The 1865 Mississippi Black Code (GMU.edu)
- Life in the South After the Civil War - Study.com
- Study.com/academy/lesson/life-in-the-south-after-the-civil-war.html
- Here are 6 Companies That Get Rich off Prisoners - Attnwww.attn.com/stories/941/who-profits-from-Prisoners
- Economic Impacts of Prison Growth - Federation of https://www.fas.org/sgp/crs/R41177Federation of American Scientists
- Racial and Ethnic Disparities in the US Criminal Justice
- Vagrancy legal definition of vagrancy - Legal Dictionary legal-dictionary.thefreedictionary.com/vagrancy
- Convict lease - Wikipedia, the free encyclopedia https://en.wikipedia.org/wiki/Convict_lease Wikipedia
- Black Lives Matter - The Schott 50 State Report on Public www.blackboysreport.org/2015-black-boys-report.pdf
- Civil Rights Act of 1964 - Wikipedia, the free encyclopedia https://en.wikipedia.org/wiki/Civil_Rights_Act_of_1964 Wikipedia
- America's War on Drugs Drives High Incarceration Rates content.time.com/time/magazine/article/0,9171,2109777,00.html
- Black Men Who Dropped Out of High School Have Very www.amren.com/.../black-men-who-dropped-out American Renaissance

- Finding Resources to Support Mentoring Programs and www.mentoring.org/old-downloads/mentoring_1154.pdf
- Stop-and-Frisk Data | New York Civil Liberties Union www.nyclu.org/.../**stop-and-frisk**-data
- Elitism Facts, information, pictures | Encyclopedia.com www.encyc
- White supremacy - Wikipedia, the freehttps://en.wikipedia.org/wiki/White_supremacy
- Cognitive dissonance - Wikipedia, the free encyclopedia
- Turf war - Wikipedia, the free encyclopedia https://en.wikipedia.org/wiki/**Turf_war**Wikipedi
- Urban Dictionary: crabs-in-a-barrel www.urbandictionary.com/define.php?...crabs-in...barr Urban Dictionary

NOTES

NOTES

www.ingramcontent.com/pod-product-compliance
Lightning Source LLC
Chambersburg PA
CBHW062118280526
45787CB00009B/276
9781522864042